WE ALL SCREAM FOR ICE CREAM!

The Scoop on America's Favorite Dessert

Withdrawn

LEE WARDLAW

Illustrated by Sandra Forrest

HarperTrophy®
A Division of HarperCollins*Publishers*

For Kristi Jensen McLoughlin,
with tasty memories of
our childhood bike trips to B & R

● ● ●

Library of Congress Catalog Card Number: 98-93663
ISBN: 0-380-80250-3

First HarperTrophy edition, 2000

❖

Visit us on the World Wide Web!
www.harperchildrens.com

j641.374
WAR

● ACKNOWLEDGMENTS ●

The author wishes to thank the following people, companies, and organizations for so generously giving her the scoop on ice cream:

Fred Borchers; Pamela Brinkworth, Communications Manager, American Dairy Queen Corporation; Sandi Bross, Brand Manager, Joy Cone Company; Susan Brunel, Eskimo Pie Corp; Hope Slaughter Bryant; Stephanie Burnham, On Any Sundae; California Milk Advisory Board; Julia Cunningham; Mitch Curren, "Info Queen & Research Relationist," Ben & Jerry's Homemade, Inc.; Les Ferreira, Ph.D., Department Head, Dairy Science Director, Dairy Products Techonology Center, California Polytechnic State University, San Luis Obispo; Janice Garrett, D.V.M.; Joe George, President, Joy Cone Company; Joan Bransfield Graham; Mary Hanson; John Harrison, Official Taste Tester, Dreyer's Grand Ice Cream; Valerie Hobbs; Gretchen Heid Homan and Beth Lyons, McDowell & Piasecki, Food Communications, Inc; *Ice Scream Magazine*; Ice Screamers; International Ice Cream Association; International Association of Ice Cream Vendors; International Dairy Deli Bakery Association; David Ivey, the Soda Fountain Website; Mary Kamm, Director, Research & Development, Ben & Jerry's Homemade, Inc.; Jill Kasser, former Media Relations Manager, Dreyer's Grand Ice Cream; Ruth Katcher; Ellen Kelley; Sharon Kolstad, Brand Manager, Good Humor-Breyers; Ginger Knowlton; Matt

v

Lamstein; Jim McCoy, President, McConnell's Fine Ice Creams; J. Sears McGee, Ph.D., University of California, Santa Barbara; Marni McGee; Lisa Merkl; National Association of Ice Cream Vendors; National Dairy Council; National Ice Cream and Yogurt Retailers Association; John Ordona, Media Relations Manager, Dreyer's Grand Ice Cream; Penn State Unversity, Ice Cream Manufacture Home Page; Dian Curtis Regan; Gary Reif, Ph.D., Dairy Science Department, Cal Poly State University, San Luis Obispo, CA; Jesse Sartain, National Director, American Tasting Institute; Harold Schuchardt; Paul and Andrea Schweikert; Vikki L. Smith, Consumer Affairs Manager, Baskin-Robbins, USA; Beth Snyder, The Ice Screamer; The Ice Cream Alliance; Bryce Thomson (Last of the Great Soda Jerks), Editor, *The Sundae School Newsletter*; Lynda Utterback, Publisher/Editor, The National Dipper; University of Guelph Food Science Home Page; April Halprin Wayland; Steve "Doc" Wilson; Karen Wood, Dippin' Flavors; Victor Zaborsky, Special Products, International Dairy Foods Association/International Ice Cream Association.

● TABLE OF CONTENTS ●

Section 1

THE ICE AGE:
Ice Cream in
Ancient History

The first cookbook in history devoted entirely to ice creams and sorbets was M. Emy's *L'art de Bien Faire les Glaces d'Office* (The Art of Making Frozen Desserts), published in France in 1768. The title page from the book illustrates a common opinion of the day that ice cream was a "food fit for the gods."

• 1 •

Ice Screamers

I scream, you scream,
We all scream for Ice Cream.
Rah! Rah! Rah!
Tuesdays, Mondays
We all scream for Sundaes.
SISS! BOOM! BAH!

—from the popular song "(I Scream—
You Scream—We All Scream for) Ice Cream"
by Howard Johnson, Billy Moll, and Robert Kin, 1927

Do *you* scream for ice cream?

If you're like most Americans, you do.

Ice cream is our nation's favorite dessert. We love to sip it in sodas, slurp it in shakes, plop it on cones, nibble it on sticks, and drown it in chocolate syrup Monday through *Sundae*. We might even eat pizza à la mode, if we could.

And then we'd ask for seconds!

According to the International Ice Cream Association (IICA), the United States makes over 1.5 *billion* gallons of ice cream a year—enough for every man, woman, and child in America to eat twenty-three quarts.

That equals 184 single-scoop cones: one a day for each of us for almost six months.

A whopping 90% of American families scream for ice cream. Kids between the ages of two and twelve are the biggest screamers, eating more than half of the ice cream sandwiches, bars, and prepackaged cones manufactured each year.

A dish of this sweet, smooth, cold-enough-to-make-your-teeth-hurt dessert has long been recognized as an American tradition. In fact, in 1921 the Commissioner of Ellis Island issued a delicious decree: all immigrants arriving in this country would receive a free scoop of ice cream with their first American meal.

Today we celebrate National Ice Cream Month and National Ice Cream Day in July. We crank out about five hundred new ice cream products every year. We produce and eat more ice cream annually than any country in the world . . . enough to fill the Grand Canyon. So you might be surprised to learn that at one time, only presidents and kings ate this frosty treat . . . and that ice cream's tasty origins date back more than two thousand years.

So read on to get the scoop, the whole scoop, and nothing but the scoop about this eleven-billion-dollar industry . . .

. . . and why everyone the world over *loves* to scream for ice cream.

Stick Out Your Tongue and Say . . . Yum!

Have you ever noticed how delicious a plain glass of cold water, with a tinkling ice cube or two, tastes on a simmering summer afternoon?

Centuries before refrigerators were invented, human beings thirsted for chilled food and drink.

"It is dangerous to heat, cool or make a commotion all

of a sudden in the body," warned the Greek doctor Hippocrates (460?–377? B.C.). But few citizens paid attention to the Father of Medicine. "Most men would rather run the hazard of their lives or health," he went on, "than be deprived of the pleasure of drinking out of ice."

Alexander the Great (356–323 B.C.), the King of Macedonia, was one such man. Tales are told of his quest to rule the world—and his passion for iced drinks. Once, during an attack on the city of Petra, Alexander ordered his army to stop the battle and dig thirty trenches, then fill them with snow brought down from the mountains. Branches were laid across the trenches to keep the snow from melting so Alexander's wines, fruits, and juices would stay cold in the hot Jordanian sun.

Roman emperor Nero Claudius Caesar Drusus Germanicus (A.D. 37–68) had a love for iced drinks and desserts that was as great as his name was long. During his cruel reign as emperor of Rome (A.D. 54–68), Nero often hosted tremendous feasts featuring wines cooled with snow and slushy honey-sweetened juices— the world's first Snow-cone!

Plans for these delicacies had to be made at least a month in advance. Nero would order slaves into the Apennine Mountains to gather snow. The weary servants were then forced to run a brutal relay race back to Rome, carting heavy loads of snow and ice through heat and many miles of treacherous terrain. The barbaric Nero, who thought nothing of killing his mother, his wife, and his teacher, once slaughtered the general in command for allowing the snow to melt before reaching the emperor's table. The slaves were boiled to death.

In this case, Hippocrates was right: frozen foods and drink could be hazardous to your health!

Got Milk?

As far back as five thousand years ago, the ancient Greeks and Eygptians milked goats, cows, and sheep. But foods made from milk, such as cheese and yogurt, did not become common until around 600 B.C. Iced dairy products made from the milk of horse, buffalo, yak, camel, cow, and goat first appeared a thousand years later during the T'ang Dynasty in China (A.D. 618-907).

Historians note that Kublai Khan, Mongol emperor of China from 1260–94, always had jars of kumiss ready for the asking. He preferred the dish to be made from the milk of pure white horses. During lavish banquets at his palace, all six thousand guests in the dining halls were ordered to kneel quietly while Kublai Khan enjoyed his dairy treat. Not a single sound, except that of his musicians playing, was permitted until the emperor had finished the last bite.

The T'ang Dynasty is known among historians of the Orient as a Golden Age of learning. Great works of poetry, literature, art, and music flourished in China at this time. Great foods must have flourished also. Emperor T'ang of Shang, founder of the dynasty, had 2,271 people on his palace cooking staff, including 94 "ice men" or ice harvesters.

Since the eighth century B.C., the Chinese had known how to harvest winter ice, storing it and keeping it cold until summer in specially designed icehouses. During the T'ang period, the ice was used for a variety of purposes, including the preparation of a frozen iced-milk product called *kumiss*.

During the hot, humid months, emperor T'ang relished eating kumiss. To make it, his chefs and ice men worked together. First, they heated or boiled the milk and fermented it. Next it was mixed with rice or flour, then combined with "dragon's eyeball powder" and "dragon's brain fragments." These last two ingredients are better

known today as camphor, a chemical taken from the wood of an evergreen tree.

The kumiss was then chilled with ice until almost frozen. The result was a cool, refreshing dish—a distant cousin to the sherbet we eat today.

Just Say Moo

Over the centuries, people in the Far East continued to create frozen dairy drinks and desserts. During the Sung Dynasty (A.D. 960–1279), Chinese author Yang Wanli (1127–1206) wrote the earliest known poem about a frozen milk product. Translated, it reads:

> *It looks so greasy but still has a crisp texture,*
> *It appears congealed and yet it seems to float,*
> *Like jade, it breaks at the bottom of the dish;*
> *As with snow, it melts in the light of the sun.*

—translated by Roderick Whitfield
Professor of East Asian Art
University of London

Some sources note that royalty and the very wealthy of India, Persia, Arabia, Turkey, and China often ate water ices, or sorbets, made with crushed ice and fragrant flowers. They also treated themselves to sherbets of frozen yak milk, sugar, and fruit pulp. These dishes were served at banquets as either an appetizer or a between-course aid to digestion. A dessert more like ice cream is also said to have been served to Chinese nobility during the Yuan Dynasty in the 1300s. Common folk never knew what they were missing. Recipes for these dairy desserts were as valuable as jewels, kept safe and secret by chefs employed in only the wealthiest of households.

The amazing traveler Marco Polo, during his visit to China in the thirteenth century, wrote of having tasted delicious sorbets and sherbets while serving as a government official in the court of Kublai Khan. When Polo returned home to Italy twenty years later, he claims to have introduced new teas and spices, a dish called spaghetti, and recipes for several frozen desserts, including one for "iced cream."

Historians argue over whether Polo's claim is true. Perhaps his recipes inspired the ice cream we delight in today. Perhaps chefs from Europe created this wintry treat on their own. No one knows for sure. Either way, there is no doubt that European royalty would soon indulge in a new frozen concoction so creamy and delicious it was revered by one Italian writer as "the flower of milk."

● 2 ●

Dessert of Kings and Queens

"After the Meat was taken off, there was served up a very fine Desert, with many great Piramids of dry Sweet-Meats, between which were placed all such Fruits, Iced Creams, and such other Varieties as the Season afforded."

—1688 London *Gazette* article describing a
royal banquet in Stockholm, Sweden

Congratulations—you're engaged to be married! You've arranged everything for the ceremony: wedding clothes, guest list, flowers, musicians.

"Oh, by the way," you say casually to your spouse-to-be. "I'd like the reception to last an entire month . . . with a different flavor of ice cream served every day."

Sound ridiculous?

Not if you were a royal teenager in sixteenth-century Italy!

Here Comes the Bride

In 1533, Catherine de Medici was a plain, petite girl of fourteen. Catherine's parents, wealthy rulers in Florence, Italy, arranged her marriage to the French Duke of

Orleans (later King Henry II). The lavish wedding festivities lasted a whopping thirty-four days. They began with a royal ball to introduce the future queen of France to her Paris court.

Self-conscious about her short, skinny figure, Catherine wanted to make an awe-inspiring impression on her subjects. First, she gave secret orders to her personal cobbler. She made a grand entrance to the ball wearing his invention: the world's first high-heeled shoes. Then, with the help of chefs brought with her from Italy, Catherine wowed her guests by serving thirty-four different sherbets and ice creams—such as lemon, lime, cherry, and wild strawberry—one for each day of her wedding party.

Although the Cinderella-like tale about Catherine's new-fangled slippers is well documented, some researchers believe the story of the parade of semi-frozen desserts is as hollow as an empty sugar cone. They point out that Catherine's confectioners would not have had access to the snow and ice needed for their recipes. However, three years before the marriage, an Italian doctor named Zimara had discovered how to make ice artificially. He published his findings in a book called *Problemata*. There is a chance, then, that Catherine's

"Food . . . which is made of milk sweetened with honey and frozen . . . some persons call it the flower of milk, some call it cream . . . "
—1560 description of Italian ice cream.

cooks had read of Zimara's discovery in time for the wedding feasts.

Off with His Head!

Another oft-told tale about ice cream's origins dates back to the seventeenth century court of Charles I.

Charles was crowned king of England, Scotland, and Ireland in 1625. Numerous books written about the history of ice cream claim that he employed a French chef, Gerard Tissain, who introduced the monarch to "crème ice." Charles enjoyed the dessert so much, he forbade Tissain to reveal the recipe to anyone.

To ensure the chef's vow of silence, Charles offered to pay "hush money:" twenty pounds a year for life. Other sources claim he spooned out five hundred pounds a year. The average seventeenth-century laborer earned only about twelve pounds annually, so Tissain's bribe was practically a king's ransom.

Since Charles I was deeply in debt for most of his reign, some historians doubt the king would have given a mere cook such a huge sum of money. But as the story goes, Tissain kept his promise—and his generous pension—until Charles was beheaded for treason in 1649. That's when the Ruler of the Recipe supposedly sold his secret. Depending on which version of this tale you believe, the recipe either passed into the hands of a group of noblemen, who had tasted ice cream at one of the king's banquets, or to several Frenchmen, who later opened a café in Paris.

Whatever the fate of the recipe, it is a fact that both sons of Charles I inherited their father's love for the dessert. At the Feast of St. George, held at Windsor Castle

in 1671, Charles II enjoyed "one plate of white strawberries and one plate of Ice Cream" two days in a row. The
king's table was the only one served these delicacies.

His brother, James II, became king a few years later.
Accounting books show that in 1686, while camped with
his army in Hounslow Heath, an area near London, James
had a dozen dishes of ice cream brought to him after a
battle. Each dish cost one pound—expensive, even for a
king. Perhaps it was extra delicious ice cream. Or, perhaps, as one historian joked: "Maybe they used big
dishes!"

Parlez-Vous Ice Cream?

Paris, France.

When you think of this romantic city, you may picture
the Eiffel Tower. Delicious pastries. Magnificent galleries.
Jaunty berets.

Paris is also the home of Café Procope: the world's
oldest operating restaurant . . . and the first to sell ice
cream.

During the early 1600s, the high cost of cream and the
difficulty of obtaining snow and ice meant that only royalty could indulge a "cold tooth." But by the middle of the
seventeenth century, iced desserts were becoming more
common among the wealthy upper class in Italy, Spain,
and France.

Francesco Procopio dei Cotelli, an Italian immigrant
from Sicily, had worked as a *limonaidier*, a lemonade
maker and salesman, during his early years in Paris. Fizzy
lemonade was popular among Parisians, and Francesco
was one of 250 master *limonaidiers* in the city. Tired of the
stiff competition, in 1686 (some sources say as early as

1660) he opened the city's first café, or coffeehouse. He dubbed it Procope—his nickname—and specialized in chocolates, perfumes, steaming-hot brews, and a frozen dessert few had ever tasted: ice cream.

Café Procope was an instant success, *the* place for high society and intellectuals to see and be seen. Francesco increased the café's popularity by selling ice cream in a variety of exotic flavors. These included chocolate, strawberry, and the little-known vanilla. Demand was so high, he had to fill large boxes with ice to keep plenty of ice cream fresh and cold for his customers.

Francesco's café was a trendsetter. Within a few years, so many copycat coffeehouses clotted the Paris streets that city officials required business owners to purchase permits before selling ice creams and sorbets. Many of the cafés developed house specialities, inventing flavors like macaroon and rum ice cream to help increase business.

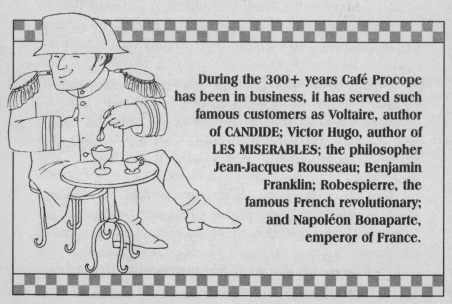

During the 300+ years Café Procope has been in business, it has served such famous customers as Voltaire, author of CANDIDE; Victor Hugo, author of LES MISERABLES; the philosopher Jean-Jacques Rousseau; Benjamin Franklin; Robespierre, the famous French revolutionary; and Napoléon Bonaparte, emperor of France.

But Francesco's creations outlasted them all, and by 1782 the café served eighty different flavors of ice cream. Café Procope remains open today, still serving hot coffee and ice cream on the Rue de l'Ancienne Comedie.

A Pinch of This, A Dash of That

Less than fifty years after the execution of Charles I, the dessert His Majesty wanted kept secret had become so popular it began to appear in cookbooks for more than just the royal chefs to read.

Lo Scalco alla Moderna, written by Antonio Latini in 1694, was the first cookbook featuring a recipe for Neapolitan sorbetti, an Italian ice cream. This dish featured two or more fruit flavors in garish colors stacked on top of each other in a brick-shaped mold. After freezing, the mold was removed and the sorbetti cut into slices like a cake.

Mrs. Mary Eale's Receipts, published in Great Britain in 1718, had two distinctions: it was the first English-language cookbook to feature an ice cream recipe, and the first cookbook ever written by a woman! (Almost all chefs at that time were men.) Mrs. Eale had served as a confectioner, or candymaker, to Queen Anne from 1702–14. The recipe, wedged between descriptions for cooking "Sego-Cream" and "Hartshorn-Flummery," required such odd yet essential ingredients as a "pound of Bay-Salt," a "Pail with Straw," and "a Cellar where no Sun or Light comes."

Two other ice cream "firsts" appeared in The Modern Cook, written by Vincent La Chapelle, head chef for England's Duke of Chesterfield. La Chapelle's book, published in 1733, was the first to include recipes using elaborate metal molds and sculpting instructions to create ice cream masterpieces. These desserts, usually served at elegant parties given by the wealthy, were works of art, as delicious as they were beautiful.

The recipes in *The Modern Cook* were the first to include directions for mixing and stirring ice cream during the freezing process. This innovative step gave the ice cream a smoother texture. Ice creams before this time were often coarse and crunchy with ice crystals.

The first cookbook in history devoted entirely to ice cream and sorbet was M. Emy's *L'art de Bien Faire les Glaces d'Office* (The Art of Making Frozen Desserts). Published in France in 1768, this hefty book contained 240 pages of recipes for apricot, violet, rose, chocolate, caramel, and other exotic ice creams.

Not much is known about the author other than that she was profoundly religious. The book included long, spiritual explanations for scientific facts such as why water freezes.

M. Emy considered ice cream holy: a "food fit for the gods." To emphasize this belief, the title page of the cookbook features an elaborate illustration of chubby-cheeked angel-babies, hard at work. One angel pushes a wheel-barrow heaped with snow. Three others labor to beat the snow and churn the ice cream, while another

"Use three pounds of ice, mix with one pound of bay salt for each pot of cream. Close pot tightly, place it inside a pail filled with ice and salt, cover pail with straw, and leave it in a dark cellar for four hours or longer."

—Recipe for ice cream, *Dictionarium Domesticum: Being a New and Compleat Household Dictionary*, by Nathaniel Bailey, London, 1736.

spoons swirls of the finished dessert into special cups. Delivery angels fly into the heavens, carefully balancing the cups on trays. Divine beings wearing robes recline in a halo of clouds, awaiting their sacred treat.

Little did Madame Emy know that science and technology—not religion—would one day bring ice cream into the homes of even the most earthly and common families.

"It is very warm here. The Viennese are afraid that it will soon be impossible to have any ice cream, for as winter is mild, ice is rare."

—German composer Beethoven, in a letter describing the Austrian winter of 1793–94.

Section 2

ICE CREAM IN THE NEW WORLD

Street peddlers—mostly poor, uneducated immigrants, former slaves, and out-of-work Civil War veterans—flooded large cities such as New York and Philadelphia in the mid-nineteenth century. Pulling ramshackle carts, they spent long summer days hawking cheap ice cream called "hokeypokey" to children of the slums. For many youngsters, a penny's worth of hokeypokey smeared on a rag or strip of paper was their first taste of what would one day become America's favorite dessert. In this 1922 photograph, a hokeypokey man sells ice cream cones from a goat-drawn wagon.

Photo credit: International Association of Ice Cream Manufacturers

• 3 •

A Presidential Treat

"Mrs. Madison always entertains with Grace and Charm, but last night there was a sparkle in her eye that set astir an Air of Expectancy among her Guests . . . in the centre [of the table] high on a silver platter [sat] a large shining dome of pink ice cream."

—description of a dinner at President Madison's
second inauguration, 1813

Cows clattered down the gangplank onto the soil of the New World in 1611, the year the Jamestown colony was established in Virginia. No one knows for sure how long the colonists used the milk for only butter and cheese. Nor is it known if it was the French, Italians, or Britains who later sailed across the Atlantic Ocean with recipes for frozen dairy desserts. But 133 years would pass between the founding of Jamestown and when ice cream was mentioned in America's history. And for many years more, it would be a delicacy that only presidents and other statesmen could afford.

"A Dessert no less Curious"

"We were received by his Excellency and his Lady in the Hall," wrote William Black in 1744, about an elegant evening at the home of Maryland's governor, Thomas Bladen. ". . . then the scene changed to a Dining Room, where you saw . . . a Table in the most Splendent manner set out with Great Variety of Dishes . . . after which came a Dessert no less Curious; some fine Ice Cream which, with the Strawberries and Milk, eat most Deliciously."

Ice cream in eighteenth-century America was a rare treat, served primarily at state or other formal dinners. The average colonist had most likely never heard of it, let alone tasted it. There were two main reasons for this.

First, the three key ingredients—sugar, cream, and ice—were scarce and expensive.

All sugar had to be imported, and most housewives kept what little they had locked in cabinets, for use only on special occasions.

During the Revolutionary War, the British slaughtered thousands of cows, making cream a "prime luxury," precious as gold.

Ice, of course, was available only in the winter. Men had to cut blocks of ice from local rivers, streams, and lakes, then keep it cold until summer in cellars and icehouses.

Second, ice cream took far too long to make. The wealthy hired servants to handle the complex and time-consuming work. But most women were too busy washing, cooking, cleaning, and caring for the children to waste precious hours making a complicated dessert that would melt in minutes.

The richest families, of course, could afford to buy ice cream in confectionary shops. In 1774, Philip Lenzi, originally a London candymaker, was the first caterer to advertise the availability of ice cream in New York City. Three years later, during the Revolutionary War, Lenzi

> At a party in 1758, Francis Fauquier, governor of Virginia, served ice cream that he made from ice gathered during a hailstorm.

tried to appease the British soldiers who had overrun the city by promising the dessert could "be had almost every day . . . executed to all perfection as in the first shops in London."

In 1779, Joseph Corre, another confectioner, advertised the sale of ice cream in the *Gazette*, a New York newspaper. Corre not only boasted that his ice cream sold for the "modest price of eleven pennies a glass," but that he was willing to deliver the confection personally—if customers ordered in advance.

Hail to the Chef!

George Washington was the first president of the United States.

He was also the first president to eat ice cream.

Researchers believe Washington may have tasted the dessert for the first time at a party in Philadelphia in July 1782. It was love at first bite. Soon after, records show that Washington bought a "cream Machine for Making Ice," two pewter ice cream pots, and an ice cream serving spoon. Martha Washington's nephew marveled at a presidential reception where "refreshments were handed round by servants in livery; and about that period first appeared the luxury, not so universal, of ice cream."

Washington was so taken with the delicious dessert that during the summer of 1790, he ordered $200 worth of ice cream: the equivalent of $96,400 today!

During his term in office (1789–97), the president and the first lady made it a practice to serve ice cream at every dinner party and afternoon levee (a type of reception). Because of Washington, DC's hot, humid summers and the lack of refrigeration, the slushy, soupy ice cream was served in china cups or saucers, and sipped daintily.

When Washington died, household records noted that the former president owned an exquisite French set of china tableware that included two dessert "iceries," twelve "ice plates" and thirty-six "ice pots." All were used for the serving of ice cream at formal affairs.

The next three presidents—John Adams, Thomas Jefferson, and James Madison—continued the tradition of serving ice cream at government functions. In fact, many of the first ice cream manufacturers and parlor operators in the country learned how to prepare the delicious dish while working as chefs at the White House.

"Officers waiting only long enough to wash away the travel stains, sat at a table to dine sumptuously on . . . dishes of ice cream, a dainty which the Army had not seen since it left the East." —Major General "Mad" Anthony Wayne, after the Battle of the Fallen Timbers, 1794.

One such cook, Augustus Jackson, became the first African-American to own an ice cream business, opening Philadelphia's original ice cream shop in 1832. He became very wealthy in this new enterprise, and later loaned money to two other black chefs to set up their own establishments.

Thomas Jefferson, in particular, helped to popularize the dessert. Known as a connoisseur of fine foods and wine, the president was always ready to sample a new delicacy. While serving as America's minister to France, Jefferson tried a wide array of ice creams, including one made with winter-fresh snow. "[It] gives the most delicate flavor to creams," he wrote, "but ice is the most powerful congealer, and lasts longer."

While in Paris, Jefferson also tasted another rarity: vanilla ice cream. He immediately concluded that, unlike men, not all ice cream flavors are created equal! He found this flavor so delectable that he brought vanilla beans home with him in the 1780s. Later, desperate for more, he imported fifty pods from Paris in 1791—giving the country its first taste of what would become the best-selling ice cream flavor of all time. The man who had penned the Declaration of Independence also wrote his own eighteen-step recipe for vanilla ice cream. In 1806 he employed a man on his presidential cooking staff whose sole job was to churn the dessert.

Dolley Madison, known in Washington society for her skills as a charming and intelligent hostess, often served elaborate ice cream desserts at dinner parties during her husband's administration, as well as for Jefferson after his wife died. Her favorite flavor was strawberry, made with fruit plucked from her garden. The cream came directly from the Madisons' own dairy.

It's a Pleasure

Two-hundred-odd years ago, girls and women didn't have the freedom to socialize outside the home. Eating in public was thought to be unladylike, so dining in a restaurant was out of the question. The theater was also unseemly. And sports? Only men were allowed to sweat! To avoid gossip, refined and fashionable ladies could only be seen in two places: churches and private homes. And they couldn't go out at all without the company of a gentleman. So most eighteenth century women were all dressed up—in white-powdered wigs and rouge-cheeked faces—with no place to go.

Until the creation of the Pleasure Gardens.

Several French confectioners, such as Joseph Corre and Joseph Delacroix, borrowed the idea for the private gardens from the popular Pleasure Parks of England. In the late 1700s, they and other confectioners built several large, meandering gardens in New York City and Philadelphia, where women and children could stroll unchaperoned along manicured paths or sit in the cool shade of trees while enjoying refreshments and entertainment. Musicians played. Fountains bubbled. Birds twittered from within gilded cages. The brave could take balloon rides. At night the sky filled with fireworks.

And there was ice cream.

The Pleasure Gardens were instrumental in giving women the freedom to venture out alone in the cities. But they also offered many women and children their first taste of ice cream. "It was the ladies, above all, who could not get enough of a pleasure so new to them as frozen food," wrote one owner of a Pleasure Garden in 1794. "Nothing was more amusing than to watch the little gri-

maces they made while savoring it. It was especially difficult for them to understand how anything could stay so
cold in the summer heat of 90 degrees."

The Pleasure Gardens were an instant hit both with
high society and with the working class. For as little as a
shilling (about twelve pennies), guests could enter to "sit
half an hour, eat ice cream, drink lemonade, hear fine
music, see a variety of people, and return home happy
and refreshed." The ice cream came in a variety of flavors:
vanilla, lemon, pineapple, strawberry, and raspberry. The
dessert became the main attraction at many of the gardens, and led to the eventual opening of "ice houses," "ice
shops," and "ice saloons"—the first ice cream parlors—in
the early 1800s.

Not everyone, however, was pleased with the Pleasure
Gardens—or the popularity of ice cream. The stuffy and
prudish thought the gardens and ice shops sinful, as they
were frequented in the evening by young men courting
their sweethearts. Other people believed, as Hippocrates
had, that eating cold foods was unhealthful. ". . . eating ice
creams, after a meal, tend[s] to reduce the temperature
of the stomach, and thus stop digestion," wrote one
disapproving matron. A newspaper cautioned readers
that the treat caused "unseemly belching." A great number
believed eating ice cream was simply frivolous. "We dare
not trust our wit for making our house pleasant to our
friend," wrote the author Ralph Waldo Emerson, "and so
we buy ice cream."

Despite the fussing of critics, the delicacy was
becoming a tradition at all social gatherings and
Independence Day celebrations. Still, ice cream was
mainly available only in large cities in the East, and its
price was out of reach for most common folk. But in 1843

a housewife would invent a device that would revolu-
tionize the freezing of ice cream, making it more acces-
sible to dessert lovers across the country.

• 4 •

The Mother of the Freezer Revolution: Nancy M. Johnson

"It is the practice of some indolent cooks to set the freezer, containing the [ice] cream, in a tub with ice and salt, and put it in the ice-house; it will certainly freeze there, but not until the water particles have subsided, and by the separation, destroyed the cream."

—Mary Randolph,
The Virginia Housewife, 1824

Can you pat your head and rub your stomach at the same time? Could you do it for two hours straight, no matter how tired your arms grew? If not, then you could never have made ice cream before the year 1843.

"[The] making of ice cream," wrote one cookbook author of that era, ". . . is an operation requiring considerable dexterity and practice."

Not to mention strong muscles!

In the eighteenth and early-nineteenth centuries, people used the "pot freezer" method to make the frozen dessert. The ingredients—cream, eggs, sugar, and flavorings—were mixed in a small tin pot or bowl, and covered tightly. The pot was placed inside a wooden bucket and surrounded with five inches or so of packed ice and salt. Then it was time to rock 'n' roll: the pot was shaken up and down while the bucket was twisted from side to side. "Keep turning the freezer . . . till the cream is frozen," recommended another cookbook in 1837, "which it will generally be in two hours."

There was no rest for the weary. If the mixture wasn't constantly shaken, and the sides of the pot weren't scraped from time to time, the cream wouldn't blend smoothly. The result would be a bowl of icy, crunchy clumps: Unappetizing, inedible, and a complete waste of rare and expensive ingredients.

Not only was the pot freezer method tricky and tedious, it required special equipment and assistance. "If mother made the custard [ice cream]," recalled one former farmboy, "the men of the household had to get the ice from the icehouse, chopping the cake out of its deep frostily steaming bed in the straw, carrying it down the ladder and cracking it up fine." Cattle salt was carted from the barn to mix with the ice to further chill it. Folded carpets wrapped around the freezer were recommended to help with insulation and to prevent spills. A candymaker from Philadelphia listed the following professional tools he deemed essential in preparing a batch of ice cream:

1. Pewter pots of various sizes . . . tin or zinc will not answer the purpose, as it congeals the mixture too quickly . . . and forms it in lumps like hailstones.
2. Moulds.
3. Ice Pails.
4. The spatula. This . . . [resembles] a gardener's spade . . . for scraping the ice cream from the sides of the pot as it freezes and for mixing it.

5. Either a large mortar and pestle, or a strong box and mallet for pounding the ice.
6. A spade wherewith to mix the ice and salt together…
7. A tin case or box for keeping the ices . . . after they are finished.

A cellar or icehouse was needed, too, for hardening and storing the ice cream. The mixture would not mold into a smooth, firm shape unless the pots were packed in straw and ice and left at brrr-cold temperatures for at least three hours after the shaking was completed.

With ice cream's popularity growing in the United States, the time was ripe for a new method that required less effort and fewer tools to create the dessert.

Enter Nancy M. Johnson.

M Is for Mystery

She is the Madam X of the ice cream world.

No one knows what she looked like, where she came from, or what became of her. We can only assume that she loved ice cream and struggled to make it the proper way, learning what a time-consuming and exhausting chore it was. Perhaps that's what led this mystery woman to design the first hand-crank freezer: a simple, practical, ingenious invention that would be the model for every home ice cream freezer sold for more than 150 years.

Some researchers claim Nancy M. Johnson was married to a naval officer; others believe her husband, Walter R. Johnson, was a professor. New Jersey and Washington, DC, both claim she resided there, although there is no proof. Even the US Patent Office was in the dark about this clever inventor, believing her to be a man, not a woman. "I had some difficulty in obtaining your letter of acknowledgment from the post office," Mrs. Johnson wrote to the patent commissioner, "in consequence of its having been directed to *Mr.* N. M. Johnson."

No surprise. It was rare in those days for a woman to design an invention, let alone file a patent for it. But the application was approved, and on September 9, 1843, *Mrs.* N. M. Johnson of Philadelphia, Pennsylvania, received a patent for what she called an "artificial freezer."

The freezer was brilliant in its simplicity: it whipped and froze the ice cream *at the same time.* It featured four main parts, which remain the standard in almost all home freezers manufactured today:

TRIPLE MOTION
WHITE MOUNTAIN
ICE CREAM FREEZER

- A tall, slim metal canister with a lid to hold the ice cream mixture.
- A revolving dasher. This is a paddlelike tool that fits inside the canister. When rotated by a crank, it mixes and beats the cream mixture and, at the same time, gently scrapes the ice cream from the walls of the canister to prevent ice crystals from forming.
- A removable crank. The crank attaches to the dasher through a small hole in the canister lid.
- A wooden tub. The canister sits inside the tub; ice and salt are layered around it.

Mrs. Johnson's innovative freezer accomplished three things:

Ice cream freezers were first patented in France in 1829. Two months before Mrs. Johnson received her US patent in 1843, Thomas Masters of England received a British patent for the first ice cream machine with a "three-bladed revolving spatula." The invention was much larger and more cumbersome than Johnson's. Masters described his creation in his 1844 publication The Ice Book, the first English cookbook to feature recipes for ice cream and water ices. Masters wrote the cookbook to help promote and sell his freezers. Seven years later, his mechanism was run by steam power and could freeze one hundred quarts of ice cream every fifteen minutes. He demonstrated it to Queen Victoria at the Crystal Palace Exhibition in June of 1851.

First, using a crank to turn the canister was far less difficult and less tiring than the potfreezer method.

Second, turning the dasher allowed the cream to freeze more evenly, and beat more air into the mixture, creating a finished product that had a smoother texture, much like fluffy mashed potatoes.

Third, the hand-crank method could shave more than an hour off the freezing time—a definite plus when children were hungry, impatient, and waiting for a taste of the treat.

A Necessary Luxury

After receiving a patent for the "artificial freezer," Mrs. Johnson did something inexplicable: she sold the rights for a mere $1500! (Some sources claim she received as little as $200.) Perhaps she needed the money. Perhaps she didn't understand the first thing about manufacturing and selling the freezers. No one knows the answer. After Mrs. Johnson sold her design to Williams & Company, a tinware business, she disappeared from the history books.

But her invention lived on . . . bringing ice cream at long last to the middle class, and inspiring the invention of more than seventy copycat freezers over the next thirty years.

Williams & Company first advertised the "Johnson Patent Freezer" in an 1845 catalog. By 1850, several similar models had hit the market. Sales were good—and so was the ice cream. *Godey's Magazine and Lady's Book*, a popular women's publication in the mid-1800s, wrote that its readers would immediately appreciate "the difference between the smooth, rich and plastic appearance of the ice cream of the present day as compared with the granular, crystalline and icy appearance" produced by the potfreezer method.

The price was right, too. Over the years, people could choose from a variety of freezers—with such wintry-sounding names as Fre-Zee-Zee, Jack Frost, The Blizzard, Polar Star, and Snow Ball—from as little as $1.15 up to $3.00. (Some super deluxe models sold for about $9.00.) So many housewives could now afford to make the dessert that the authors of *The American Woman's Home* complained: "there are more women . . . who can furnish you with a good ice cream than a well-cooked mutton chop."

Ice cream had become "one of the necessary luxuries of life," insisted *Godey's*. At parties and other social events, "nothing [could] supply the place of ice-cream. It would be like breakfast without bread, or dinner without a roast."

In 1883, cookbook author Maria Parloa wrote: "An ice cream freezer is a great luxury in a family, and will soon do away with that unhealthy dish—pie. No matter how small the family, nothing less than a gallon freezer should be bought, because . . when you have friends in, there is no occasion to send to the confectioner's for what can be prepared as well at home."

The most appealing feature to buyers of the patent freezers was how fast and easily they could produce the dessert. "In its operations it is plain, simple and uniform, and requires no looking after," announced an ad for the Massers's Self-Acting Patent Ice Cream Freezer and Beater. "All can be performed by a child of 12 years, by simply turning a crank." Many manufacturers boasted their machines could crank out a batch of ice cream in as little as twenty, ten, five . . . even two minutes! But not all these claims proved true. Elizabeth Prentiss, a young girl in the 1850s, would later recall her family's first experience with a two-minute freezer:

> We celebrated the glorious Fourth [of July] by making and eating ice-cream . . . We screwed [the freezer] to the wood-house floor . . . put in the cream, and the whole family stood and watched Papa while he turned the handle. At the end of two minutes we unscrewed the cover and gazed inside, but there were no signs of freezing, and to make a long story short . . . there we all were from half-past twelve to nearly two o'clock, when we decided to have dinner and leave the servants to finish it. It came on the table at last, very rich and rather good.

Despite improvements made in Johnson's design, ice cream was still far from fast food . . . especially since the colder the dessert froze, the harder it was to turn the crank. "Forethought was essential, and physical exertion," reminisced one man who grew up making ice cream on the family farm at the turn of the twentieth century. Back then, the bulk of the cranking was done by children: Each child, he said, "had to stand his trick at the freezer, and how long it took! Turning in the morning, with the funny paper to help; turning in the forenoon, while everybody was at church; making the last slow, weary yet thrilling revolutions . . . And then at last the reward, worth almost any travail, of licking off that delicious, thickly dripping wooden [dasher] and of thinking about saucersful still to come!"

Companies continued to experiment with creative methods to cut down on the cranking time and effort. The manufacturer of the American Twin Freezer boasted that not only could you make *two* flavors at once in its apparatus, but absolutely no cranking was necessary: only a gentle rocking back and forth motion. "It is very much less tiresome than turning a crank round and round," advertisements claimed, "[as] one can sit back in a chair with freezer alongside and rock the crank to and fro without discomfort or undue exertion."

There were, of course, fuddy-duddies in every crowd, resistant to change and suspicious of any new-fangled bit of machinery. These people scoffed at crank freezers. One cookbook recommended buying a patent freezer only if you wanted to make ice cream on short notice. "For common use," the author advised, "an old-fashioned one is the best, especially as servants are apt to get a patent freezer out of order."

The most famous freezer company in the world is White Mountain, which began producing hand-crank ice cream freezers in 1853. Founded by Thomas Sands in Laconia, New Hampshire, the company later moved to Nashua, where the highest quality New England pine was used for its superinsulated wooden tubs. Skilled European artisans and woodworkers were hired to design the soon-to-be famous "Triple Motion Freezer", which featured two dashers that turned in opposite directions while the canister revolved as well. The company also owned its own foundry where every single part of the freezer was constructed. White Mountain freezers are still available today, and are considered the crème de la ice crème in the world of frozen dessert. Many of White Mountain's employees are the great-grandchildren of the original workers at the factory.

What Goes Around, Comes Around

Eventually, larger patent freezers were designed for use at ice cream plants. Horses did all the legwork: hitched to treadmills, they powered a tangle of pulleys and drive belts that turned the freezer cranks, producing forty quarts of the delicacy in one batch. By the 1900s, horses were replaced by steam boilers and gasoline engines to run what were called "power freezers." From 1912–28, the Sears & Roebuck catalog advertised the "Auto Vacuum" ice cream freezer. Housewives poured the cream mixture into a special compartment built inside a can that held salt and ice. The can was then strapped to the running board—a long footstep—of a Model A car. Since roads back then were usually unpaved and rocky, the bumpity-bump motion of a long drive provided families with instant ice cream at their destination!

Most of the home patent freezers, however, remained unchanged. There was little manufacturers could do to improve Nancy Johnson's perfect design, and by 1905 only fourteen freezer companies remained in business. When the first electric home freezer came on the market in 1930, ice cream lovers were thrilled. But since the innovative freezers cost almost $30—an exorbitant amount during the Great Depression—most families stuck with the hand-cranked models that still sold for only about $3.00.

Today, in the twenty-first century, hand- and power-crank home freezers are considerably more expensive, ranging in price from $25 up to $1,000. But whether they are made of space-age materials or the still-dependable wood, or whether they feature chemicals, electric refrigeration, or the tried-and-true ice-and-salt combo, the principle behind them has remained the same for over a century and a half.

Nancy M. Johnson's simple invention pulled ice cream out of the elite deep freeze and into the homes of the common folk. Within eight years of its creation, the "artificial freezer" would crank up the commercial ice-cream-making industry that would soon expand nationwide and beyond . . .

Take two scoops and call me in the morning . . .
Steve Wilson, a doctor in Fayetteville, Arkansas, is listed in the 1999 Guinness Book of World Records as owning the largest antique ice cream freezer collection on the planet: 160 freezers in all! The oldest and rarest—a combination freezer and butter churn—dates back to around 1865. He also owns a Fre-Zee-Zee from 1871. Doc Wilson keeps about 60 of his freezers on display in a special "ice cream room" in his home. "They must be dusted frequently," he says, "a big job! To keep them in shape, the old ice-and-salt freezers must also be used from time to time." Among his unique collection is the world's smallest steam-driven ice cream freezer, "which makes only 1 cup of ice cream and is run by a tiny steam engine." He also owns a Kenmore electric freezer from the 1950s. The freezer has a voice box that announces "Your Kenmore Ice Cream Freezer is now working!" and "Your ice cream is now ready!" The doctor has made a variety of flavors in his freezers but, he says, vanilla will always be his favorite. The weirdest flavor he's ever made? Pickle!

• 5 •

The Father of the American Ice Cream Industry: Jacob Fussell

Descending into the cellar work room of the typical ice cream factory, the visitor finds himself surrounded by countless boxes, vats, tanks, casks or other receptacles filled with ice, near which are groups of busy workers preparing the rich raw cream for the freezers . . . then whippers are inserted into the cans, the covers clamped tightly on, and the cans attached to the machinery. A rasping squeak, a subdued roar, a crushing, grinding noise of ice, and the cans are whirling furiously in their icy bed . . . this continues for ten minutes, when the cans are removed to make way for others.

—Ice & Refrigeration, 1892

His eight children loved him as an avid storyteller. Businessmen thought him a hardworking penny-pincher. Fellow Quakers knew his quiet, peace-loving side. Runaway slaves welcomed his help along the Underground Railroad.

But today, Jacob Fussell is best remembered as the Father of the American Ice Cream Industry.

A Quaker's Life

Jacob Fussell (rhymes with "muscle") was born in Little Falls, Maryland, on February 24, 1819. His family, members of the Society of Friends, or Quakers, had traveled to the New World from England in the early 1700s. Wanting the freedom to live according to their beliefs, many Quakers had journeyed to America at that time to avoid religious persecution.

Young Jacob grew up a devout, soft-spoken boy, spending much time in quiet meditation. He spoke in the manner typical of Quakers in those days, using "thou" and "thee" instead of "you" in his conversations. He learned to be frugal with his money, and was taught that violence and slavery were evil.

The latter view was a rarity where Jacob lived. Before the Civil War began in 1861, most households in the Southern United States owned black slaves. Maryland, Jacob's home, was known as a Border State: a Slave State located in the north next to a Free State.

Over the years, members of the Fussell family worked as farmers or tradesmen. Jacob was no exception. When he reached his teen years, his parents signed a contract agreeing to have their son serve as an apprentice to a stove fitter, a man who built and installed cooking stoves. Early in the nineteenth century, teenage boys commonly left the family home for two or three years to work for a master craftsman. In exchange, the boys received training in a particular trade—such as woodworking or blacksmithing—and free room and board.

When Fussell finished his apprenticeship, he decided to open his own stove fitting business. Although he prided himself as a good businessman—keeping detailed, daily records of every penny spent—his company eventually failed.

An older Quaker friend came to the rescue. The friend had loaned money to a man who ran an ice cream catering and milk delivery business. Unable to repay the loan, the dairyman gave his business to the friend. The friend had no interest in, or knowledge of, running this kind of company. Would Fussell be willing to try it? With no other options, Fussell readily agreed.

A Perfect Fit

Surprisingly, the former stove fitter found his new career to be a perfect fit. He enjoyed the popularity of being one of the new "urban dairymen." These were men who lived in the city. They owned no cows or milking pails. Instead, they bought milk daily from farmers.

Every morning, Pennsylvania farmers would rise in the chilly darkness to milk their cows. Cans of milk were then loaded hurriedly onto wagons and driven over bumpy, dirt roads to reach the nearest train station before sunrise. By 5 A.M., hundreds of large milk containers were aboard the train bound for Baltimore, Maryland. Fussell and his fellow dairymen met the incoming train with wagons and set out immediately to deliver milk to their customers.

City buyers loved the farm-fresh milk. In the days before railroads, country milk could not be transported to the cities by wagon or cart. The journey took far too long, and the milk arrived curdled and spoiled. So for a time, dairymen in New York, Boston, and other large cities kept their cows in urban stables. Many of these stables were unsanitary, and the cattle often sickened from the lack of

In London, England, in the early to mid-nineteenth century, urban dairymen—also known as cowkeepers—often added hot water to unsanitary milk, advertising it as "warm from the cow."

fresh air, grass, and grain. Unscrupulous dairymen fed their cows garbage and food scraps mixed with water. Others gave them slop—used grains—left over from distilleries (factories that make alcohol). These cows produced "swill milk," which was so thin and watery that some dairymen added plaster of Paris or chalk dust to whiten the liquid.

Doctors and medical reformers eventually exposed these dairies as being a dangerous health risk, especially to babies and children who drank the most milk. One by one, the facilities were closed down. Once the railroads expanded to the outlying towns and farms, and ice was used to refrigerate milk during the journey, the remaining city dairies dried up.

A Tasty Change

By the winter of 1851, when Fussell was thirty-two, he had four successful dairy delivery routes in Baltimore. He also had a big problem: customers frequently bought cream, but Fussell never knew from day to day how much they would need. Remember: Alexander Graham Bell would not invent the telephone for another twenty-five years. So people could not call Fussell before he left in the early morning to say: "No cream today." This meant that gallons of cream often had to be thrown away.

What a waste of money—and of a good product!—thought Fussell. Then he came up with a plan. He'd been running the ice cream business on the side, catering to special parties and events. Why not turn the extra cream into . . . ice cream!

Fussell figured that if he opened a factory and manufactured large quantities of ice cream, he could afford to sell the treat for 25 cents a quart: 40 cents less than its price in confectioner shops.

That winter, in Seven Valleys, Pennsylvania, Fussell harvested enough river ice to fill a large icehouse. There it would be stored and kept frozen until summertime. (In those days, unlike today, ice cream was a seasonal food, selling mostly in the scorching months of June, July, and August.) He then started construction of America's first commercial ice cream factory.

On June 15, 1851, the factory opened, and Fussell began production. He made his first batch of ice cream the old-fashioned pot-freezer way—using two dishpans!

In the beginning, Fussell produced mere scoops of ice cream: only about two quarts a day. Then he tried advertising his product, calling himself a "country produce dealer" who promised to sell "ice cream at 25 cts. per quart, delivered in moulds or otherwise, day or night."

Business took off. Soon, Fussell was able to buy more sophisticated hand-crank freezers and make ice cream in bulk.

At first, Fussell worked alone in his factory, or with one or two occasional helpers. This would be common practice among small ice cream companies until the turn of the twentieth century. During the frenzied summer months, manufacturers typically labored six days a week, twelve to fourteen hours a day. On Sunday, they finally had time off—after working till noon, of course. One small plant owner, Morris Lifter, recalled his hectic schedule: "[I would have to] get up in the morning, make the fire under the boiler, feed and curry the horse, make the [ice cream] mix, and if I was not actually freezing the cream, I was delivering it."

As the popularity of Fussell's ice cream grew, so did his factory. Dozens of workers were hired to hand-crank dozens of patent freezers. Fussell's tasty change in

When Jacob Fussell began the US ice cream industry in 1851, the average American ate less than one teaspoon of ice cream a year.

careers stood on the brink of becoming a monumental success.

For the next two years, Fussell produced batches upon batches of ice cream, packing it in ice to be shipped to Baltimore by way of the Northern Central Railroad. Eventually, though, he found it too difficult to keep an eye on the increasing production at the plant, in addition to his sales and delivery duties in the city. So, in 1853, Fussell moved his factory to Baltimore.

Although the move increased manufacturing costs, sales boomed. By 1856, Fussell had built a second plant in Washington, DC, and a third opened its doors in Boston in 1862. A New York City factory—the first of its kind in the Big Apple—followed in 1863. It eventually employed

250 workers and serviced customers with 250 delivery wagons. In 1893, thirty years after its grand opening, 60 percent of the ice cream eaten in that city was made in Fussell's original New York plant.

A Man of Integrity

In the late 1800s, large ice cream factories like Fussell's used over 100,000 pounds of ice every day during the summer months.

Although people loved Fussell's ice cream, not everyone loved Jacob Fussell himself.

A group of businessmen from the Associated Confectioners of New York frowned on his practice of selling ice cream at such a low, competitive price. They feared customers might only buy Fussell's inexpensive products, driving confectioners out of business.

One day several committee members visited Fussell's office unannounced. They issued this warning: If he didn't sign a paper agreeing to "fix" his price at $1.25 a quart—meaning, charge the same as most confectioners—they would ruin his business. Fussell was

Americans ate about four thousand gallons of ice cream in 1859, the first year the US kept records about ice cream consumption. By the end of the century, Americans would be eating five million gallons annually.

appalled. He was doing very well selling ice cream for 60 cents a quart. How dare these men tell him how to run his company! He refused to sign the paper, and threw the confectioners out of his office. They left, furious and flustered, but never followed through on their threats.

In the years before and during the Civil War, Fussell's politics often got him into trouble.

From an early age, Fussell had been an abolitionist: a person who crusaded to end the practice of slave ownership in America. His Quaker upbringing and the Declaration of Independence both taught that all men are created equal. Fussell believed in this principle with a passion. He opened his home as a station along the Underground Railroad, offering food and temporary shelter to escaping slaves as they made their way to the Free States and Canada.

As part of the abolitionist movement, Fussell frequently gave fire-and-brimstone speeches, preaching his radical, unpopular beliefs to Southerners and slaveholders whenever he could. Crowds of people gathered round to hear the normally soft-spoken man. The louder his words, the more angry the crowd became. The angrier the crowd, the more daring and defiant Fussell grew. Once, he so upset his audience they threatened violence. A lynch mob was formed. Rope in hand, they crashed through the door of his Maryland office, ready to hang him from the nearest tree. Fussell managed to escape, slipping out the back door just in the nick of time.

After this experience, Fussell became an ardent supporter of Abraham Lincoln. He served as a delegate to the Republican convention where Lincoln was nominated for president. The two later became good friends. When the

Civil War began, sutlers—people who followed the Northern army to sell food and drink to the soldiers—offered to buy every scoop of ice cream from Fussell's Washington factory. Although fiercely loyal to Lincoln and the Union, Fussell refused. He chose instead to sell only to his regular customers, believing they would be more loyal to his product—and better about paying their bills.

A Memorial to an Industry

In the years after the Civil War, Jacob Fussell increased the size of his plants, adding more freezers and hiring more help. He took on several partners, opening Jacob Fussell & Company in 1870. He shared his vast knowledge about the ice cream industry, teaching others how to make commercial ice cream. Soon, factories similar to Fussell's opened in St. Louis, Missouri; Cincinnati, Ohio; Chicago, Illinois; Lawrence, Kansas; and Philadelphia, Pennsylvania.

Fussell was also instrumental in starting the first ice cream factory in South America. When Frederic Tudor, owner of a gigantic ice export company in Boston, wanted to expand his business to other countries, he made Fussell an incredible offer: If Fussell would agree to build an icehouse and ice cream factory in Brazil, Tudor would write him a blank check. Fussell replied with a resounding No. Instead, he agreed to train one of Tudor's employees to undertake the project. His fee? A mere $500. After a crash course in ice cream making, the employee set sail, and soon established Tudor's plant in Rio de Janeiro. Fussell was relieved. The job would have taken him too far away from his eight children. He also did not want to "depart from a land where dollars were plenty, and yellow fever unknown."

Dollars were indeed plenty for Fussell. His ice cream factories made him an extremely wealthy man. Fussell gave a great deal of his money to charity. One of his favorite projects was Fussell Court, a redbrick housing development built for newly freed slaves. The homes were completely funded by Fussell.

When Jacob Fussell died in 1912 at the age of ninety-three, the ice cream industry he had created had grown from two quarts a day to almost 150 million gallons a year.

In June of 1951, the city of Baltimore and the International Association of Ice Cream Manufacturers (IAICM) hosted the centennial celebration of America's first ice cream factory. Bands played, songs were sung, proclamations read, speeches were made. And every child received a free dish of ice cream.

To cheers and applause, Senator Herbert R. O'Conor of Maryland gave the final stirring, patriotic speech. He praised Jacob Fussell for starting an industry which "could only happen in America . . . [the product of] individual initiative and private enterprise." Because of Fussell, he proclaimed, ice cream had become "an integral part of the American way of life."

Then, as a final honor, Carrie Fussell Craft, Fussell's eighty-four-year-old daughter, unveiled a simple but elegant bronze plaque. Planted in concrete on the corner of Hillen and Exeter Streets, the plaque can still be seen today. It reads:

On this site Jacob Fussell in 1851 established the first wholesale ice cream factory in the world. This was the foundation of a major American industry devoted to the production of one of the most wholesome, nutritious and popular foods.

• 6 •

Hokeypokey Men: The First Ice Cream Vendors

In summer when the sun is high,
And children's lips are parched and dry,
An ice is just the thing to try.
So this young man who comes, 'tis plain,
From Saffron Hill or Leather Lane,
A store of pence will quickly gain.
"A lemon ice for me," says Fred;
Cries Sue, "No, have a cream instead."
"A raspberry!" shouts Newsboy Ned.
"What fun! Although we're now in June,
It feels" —says Ned—"this afternoon,
Like eating winter with a spoon!"

—"The Penny-Ice Man"
anonymous, mid-nineteenth century

"Do the hokeypokey!" You probably know the words and even the easy dance steps to this old song. But what you might *not* know is that "hokeypokey" was once a name for ice cream . . . and that peddlers sold it to crowds of poor children on the streets of nineteenth-century England and America.

Pinching Pennies

Records show that street vendors sold ice cream and fruit ices in New York City, London, and Paris as early as the 1820s. By the 1840s, there were thirty thousand of them—many of whom also sold matches, clothes, and flowers—in London alone. The peddlers carried kettles of "penny licks," small crystal glasses filled with a dollop of ice cream or sorbet. No spoon was needed: Customers simply sucked or licked the treat from the tiny goblets. The cost? A half-penny to a penny. The vendors were therefore called Penny-Ice Men.

In 1865, city streets suddenly swelled with new armies of vendors in both the US and Great Britain. This happened for three reasons.

First, Nancy Johnson's hand-cranked ice cream freezer had made the production of ice cream easier and cheaper. The frozen dessert was no longer an elite treat. Now just about anyone could make it, and even the poorest of children could afford a penny's worth.

Second, when the American Civil War ended in April 1865, thousands of veterans and former slaves no longer had homes or work. To make ends meet, they flooded the cities, hawking inexpensive ice cream and other cheap confections to children.

Third, unhappy in their homeland because of political and economic problems, Italians immigrated to England and America by the thousands in the mid-nineteenth century. Mostly poor, uneducated, and unskilled—except in the family tradition of making ice cream—these young men found they could scratch out a meager living by selling the popular dessert in the streets and slums. So many hokeypokey vendors filled the streets of England in the late-nineteenth century that there was no market for factory-made ice cream, and the commercial ice cream industry in Great Britain was delayed for decades.

I Scream, Ice Cream!

"Ecco un poco! Che un poco!" sang the Italian vendors as they pulled their carts of ice cream through the streets. American and English children didn't understand the foreign words, which meant "Here's a little! Oh, how cheap!" Instead, the unfamiliar phrases ran together in their ears to sound like "hokeypokey," and many historians believe that's how the ice cream got its name.

The vendors soon picked up on the singsong rhyme and created new calls to advertise their products: "Hokeypokey, sweet and cold; for a penny, new or old!" or "Hokeypokey, find a cake; hokeypokey on the lake!" (These jingles would later become jump-rope rhymes.) Others simply bellowed: "I scream, ice cream!" They also rang bells to attract attention, a sales tactic the Good Humor men would find equally successful in the 1920s.

Children loved hokeypokey, and on hot days would swarm around the ice men as early as 7 A.M, pulling pennies from their pockets for a smear of ice cream on a rag or rip of paper. (One Italian vendor claimed to have sold more than forty gallons of the frosty treat every day during the summer months.) The upper and middle classes looked down their noses at these ragamuffins and their parents. "Thriftless, but affectionate, is the lower class parent," huffed one newspaper editorial. "Shoes the child must do without, for the father has not quite enough money to purchase them. But here is five cents to buy a hokeypokey. That much he can afford."

Hokeypokey featured three flavors in one square slice, and was described in the 1895 book *Old London Street Cries* as being "dreadfully sweet, dreadfully cold and hard as a brick." It was supposedly made from milk, condensed milk, sugar, vanilla, cornstarch and gelatin— but was rumored actually to contain sour milk and turnip pulp.

Living in slums, the hokeypokey men were forced to make their products under unsanitary conditions. And there was no way to wash up while they were selling on the streets. After each use, the penny-lick glasses were dipped in a pail of cold water and wiped with the vendor's dirty towel—the same towel used to wipe hundreds of other glasses that day. These unhealthful habits contaminated the ice cream, which often caused stomachaches and diarrhea. This led children to revise their rhymes to: "Hokeypokey, a penny a glass. Fall fresh from the donkey's ass!" and "Hokeypokey, a penny a lump. The more you eat, the more you jump!"

In 1901, these ice cream scandals were investigated by two of London's most respected chemists. They took samples of hokeypokey ice cream and the wash water, examined and analyzed them under a microscope, and published the appalling findings:

". . . [in the ice cream we found] human hair, coal dust, fragments of bed straw, hair of dogs and cats, sour crusts, fleas, bugs and many other nauseating articles. . . [in the water we found] an evil-smelling, thickish and slimy liquid, full of bacteria and sediments, including, of course, saliva from the many mouths that had touched the glasses during the day."

Disgusted, the London County Council enacted a

number of health rules, regulations, and licensing requirements for the street vendors. Unscrupulous and impoverished vendors were forced to close down. But other hokeypokey dealers met the new standards and continued to sell "che un poco" until well into the 1920s. The penny licks were finally banned in 1926 because of outbreaks of contagious diseases such as tuberculosis.

A Hard Life

An American cookbook, published in 1892, featured a delicious recipe for lemon hokeypokey that could be found "on the New York streets [sold by] the sons of sunny Italy." But the lives of most hokeypokey men were far from sunny—especially since many were not men at all.

According to a New York City guidebook published in the late 1800s, women ". . . from the oldest gray-haired grandmother, tottering on her cane, down to the young woman of sixteen" sold hokeypokey. So did "numerous little girls, struggling to get a living . . . from three-years-old and up." Midgets and the handicapped, who found it difficult to find jobs because of biases against their height or special needs, also took to the streets with pails and carts of ice cream. But the vast majority of vendors were young boys, newly arrived in this country from Italy, Ireland, and Greece, many of whom had few English skills and even less money.

A typical day for hokeypokey boys began before dawn. They awoke "huddled together, mostly in the poorer quarters of town" in "overcrowded and unsanitary conditions," explained P. Michaels in his 1910 book *Ices and Soda Fountain Drinks*. Their parents or bosses would send them out early, forcing them to walk miles to buy ice and rock salt needed in the making of hokeypokey. Upon returning, they wearily hand-cranked the ice cream for what seemed like hours, "either in badly ventilated sheds . . . or on the pavements themselves, and then dragged their heavy [wheel]barrows, on a semi-empty stomach" along their routes far across town.

Some of the kinder bosses let the boys use the wheelbarrows, wagons, or small goat-pulled carts for free. Most, however, charged rent: at least $1.50 a day. Since hokeypokey vendors often earned a daily wage of just under $5.00—and more than half of that went toward ice cream and the bosses' percentage—the boys earned less than $1.00 for sixteen hours of work. (Vendors typically sold ice cream up until 9 P.M. in the summer.) To make ends meet in cold weather when ice cream sales were sluggish, the boys sold roasted chestnuts, yams, and potatoes. In Los Angeles, they sold Mexican tamales.

Out on the streets, hooligans and gangs of older boys often teased and taunted the youngest hokeypokey vendors. They also broke the penny-lick glasses, threw horse dung and dirt into the ice cream freezers, and stole the day's meager earnings. When the boys returned home empty-handed, they were often cursed, kicked, and beaten—then sent out again the next morning to begin the cycle once more.

After one nasty beating, a young hokeypokey vendor could take the abuse no longer: he stabbed his boss to death with an ice pick. The murder made headlines, and led to an investigation into the street production and sales of ice cream—and the poor treatment of its child-vendors. Mary Engle Pennington, head of a Philadelphia bacteriological lab, led a crusade to teach the hokeypokey peddlers sanitary habits, such as washing their equipment in boiling water. The lessons worked: inspections increased, and conditions improved.

The hokeypokey men disappeared almost completely, both here and abroad, by the 1920s. Soda fountains had replaced them in popularity, and the Good Humor vendors, with their sterling reputations for high quality, service and conduct, began to make the rounds on the streets of America. In England, Wall's ice cream products, similar to Good Humor, became trendy, as their vendors wheeled giant tricycles around town, towing ice cream carts bearing signs that read: "Stop me and buy one!"

> "Some of these [hokey-pokey] men are . . . able-bodied fellows, quite strong and healthy enough to be clearing up land in the West or laying bricks at five dollars a day. For some unaccountable reason, they prefer to remain in New York, living from hand to mouth and doing nothing to improve themselves mentally, worldly or financially."
>
> —A New York City guide book, circa late 1800s.

As jobs grew scarce in the 1930s, hokeypokey peddlers popped up again for a short while during the Great Depression. An ice cream substitute called Hokeypokey went on the market in Great Britain during World War II when the manufacturing of ice cream was banned. Otherwise, all that remains of the hokeypokey men are a few grainy, black-and-white photographs and the child-hood memories of great-grandparents who enjoyed the cold penny-a-lump treats of bygone days.

Vendors who walk the streets selling ice cream still exist in large cities around the world. Many of the 400,000 Haitian immigrants in Venezuela have become heladeros and heladeras—ice cream men and women—selling the popular EFE brand of helado (ice cream) to earn money for their impoverished families still living in the Caribbean. Most use pushcarts or carry heavy ice cream boxes on their backs. They work twelve hours a day, earning from $10–$40. The job is exhausting and dangerous—many get robbed trudging home in the dark. "Oh, those hills are big," sighs one heladera at the end of a long day. "But at least the cart is empty."

• 7 •

A History Mystery: The Origins of the Ice Cream Cone

**"Oh, sure. She's the lady holding up
the ice cream cone!"**

—An eight-year-old boy's answer to the question:
"Can you describe the Statue of Liberty?"

The St. Louis World's Fair!

From April through November 1904, twenty million people visited this colossal fair, meandering through 142 miles of exhibits, shows, and concessions. They tapped their feet to the marching music of John Philip Sousa's Military Band. They shivered with patriotism at displays of the Liberty Bell and the original log cabin where Abraham Lincoln was born. They *oohed* and *aahed* at the first demonstration of cooking with electricity, and swooned at the dizzying height of the gargantuan Observation Wheel (later known as the Ferris wheel).

They also nibbled, licked, and crunched a brand-new treat dubbed the "World's Fair Cornucopia": America's first ice cream cone!

But who invented the cone? How was it invented . . . and why?

Here's the scoop on the origins of the ice cream cone . . .

The St. Louis World's Fair celebrated the hundredth anniversary of the Louisiana Purchase. In 1803, the United States paid France $15 million to buy the Louisiana Territory, which stretched from the Mississippi River to the Rocky Mountains and from the northern tip of British North America to the Gulf of Mexico. This purchase doubled the size of the US and eventually led the country to expand its borders clear to the Pacific Ocean.

Waffley Good!

For five decades, the history of the ice cream cone remained a mystery. Several gentlemen who had made their fortunes in the cone manufacturing business took credit for this simple yet innovative invention. But who was the real inventor? All insisted their stories were true. All their stories sounded believable.

In 1954, in honor of the cone's fiftieth birthday, the International Association of Ice Cream Manufacturers (IAICM) hosted its annual convention in St. Louis, Missouri. As part of the two-day conference, they met with the cone makers' relatives to try to solve the mystery, once and for all.

After listening to hours of testimony, the IAICM finally made a decision. They reasoned that a number of concession stand operators probably had come up with the idea for a cone at about the same time. After all, the Fair had boasted at least fifty ice cream stands. But, in the end, the strongest evidence pointed to an immigrant from the Persian Gulf: Ernest A. Hamwi.

Hamwi, who grew up in Damascus, Syria, traveled to the United States in 1903. To earn money in his new country, Hamwi opened a food booth at the St. Louis World's Fair. He sold a dessert, popular in his homeland, called *zalabia*: thin, crisp waffles sprinkled with sugar. Hamwi cooked each *zalabia* on a flat waffle iron, heated in an oven over a bed of coals.

The *zalabia* sold well, and for good reason: Hamwi's booth stood along The Pike, an amusement highway that traveled the entire center length of the fairgrounds. Visitors could munch Hamwi's pastry while strolling along The Pike, stopping to watch performers and exotic animals at featured shows, or touring exhibits such as replicas of Ancient Rome and the Tyrolean Alps.

Hamwi's booth stood next to a vendor who sold ice cream. One scorching day, two of Hamwi's workers noticed something unusual: after buying *zalabia*, several customers hurried to the ice cream booth next door to plop a cool scoop atop the hot waffle. They thought this combination sounded tasty, and told Hamwi what they had seen. Inspired, Hamwi whisked the next waffle off the iron and, being careful not to burn his fingers, quickly shaped it into a funnel. He filled the funnel with ice cream and the ice cream cone was born.

Word of the "World's Fair Cornucopia"—named because the curled pastry resembled a horn of plenty—spread faster than a bowl of ice cream melts in the sun. People loved the cornucopias. Not only did they taste good, but they were an edible dish. No longer would customers have to take the time to finish their dessert at a booth before continuing on their way. Even better for the

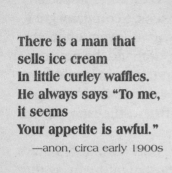

There is a man that
sells ice cream
In little curley waffles.
He always says "To me,
it seems
Your appetite is awful."

—anon, circa early 1900s

vendors: no dishes to wash! Within a few days, Hamwi was taking orders and selling his folded waffles to almost every ice cream vendor in the park.

Movin' on . . .

When the St. Louis World's Fair closed November of 1904, Ernest Hamwi started the Cornucopia Waffle Oven Company. (The new ice cream holders would not be called "cones" until 1906.) But he tired quickly of manufacturing waffle makers, and soon went to work for the competition: Heckle's Cornucopia Waffle Oven Company of St. Louis. At Heckle's he used his expertise as the cone's inventor to help promote America's new treat. He traveled hundreds of miles across the South, introducing the ice cream cone to people in Florida, Georgia, South Carolina, and Texas. To help with publicity, he arranged with J.P. Heckle to give away free samples by the thousand at county fairs, political rallies, amusement parks,

The Star Bottling Company supplied the fifty ice cream booths at the Fair with more than five thousand gallons of ice cream every day.

community picnics, and other outdoor events.

Hamwi's publicity stunts worked. Children especially liked the easy-to-hold cones, and Heckle's company grew. Heckle had bought Hamwi's original oven after the World's Fair. To meet the increasing demand, he now perfected the design, creating special ovens that could heat three waffle irons at the same time. He also hired more workers. Cornucopia makers during the early 1900s employed mostly young women to hand-roll the waffles as they came steaming out of the ovens. Each girl could roll about 1,500 waffles a day, and earned between 20 and 35 cents per stack of one hundred cones. The cones sold to vendors for a penny apiece. Vendors, in turn, sold the cones topped with ice cream for 5 cents.

Eventually, Hamwi chose to run his own cone business again. In 1910 he opened the Missouri Cone Company of St. Louis. According to Hamwi's nephew, for the next thirty-three years Hamwi "engineered and built all kinds of cone machines" and his wife "handled the money." The Cone King died in 1943, a very wealthy man.

Creative Abe

Another "waffles to cones" success story belongs to Abe Doumar.

In 1904, Doumar had recently arrived in St. Louis from Lebanon, a country in the Middle East. He got a job at the World's Fair selling paperweights in an exhibit called the Ancient City of Jerusalem. At the end of the day when his booth closed, Doumar often liked to hang out at the fairgrounds. Rather than go home to his twelve brothers and sisters, he stayed late watching belly dancers or nibbling dessert waffles. (Some accounts claim he spent a lot of time at Hamwi's *zalabia* stand.)

In Lebanon, Doumar had enjoyed the custom of eating pita bread filled with jam. He mentioned this to one waffle vendor, and suggested the man fill *zalabia* with ice cream instead. The vendor tried it, people loved it, and profits soared. Impressed, he offered Doumar a part-time job working at the booth. When the Fair closed a few months later, the appreciative vendor gave Doumar one of his waffle ovens as a thank-you present.

Doumar, who had a sharp mechanical mind, tinkered with the oven, improving its design. With the help of three partners, he soon moved to New York and set up an ice cream business at Coney Island. There he sold cones from a stand near Steeplechase Park.

Business boomed. On cool days, when sales slacked off, Doumar used pretty girls as a walking advertisement. The girls were paid to meander up and down the board-walk, eating cone after cone with delight. The stunt worked, and sales always increased.

As time went on, Doumar expanded his business. He took to the road, traveling great distances to run ice cream cone stands at amusement parks and state fairs. Later he set up each of his brothers and sisters in their own ice cream businesses. Doumar's Drive-In Restaurant in Norfolk, Virginia, opened in the

1930s, specializing in ice cream cones and barbecued foods. The drive-in did well until the 1950s. That's when a new fast-food restaurant came to town. Its instant popularity almost forced Doumar's to close its doors.

Then Abe's relatives came up with a clever plan. They dusted off their ancestor's ancient waffle oven, cleaned it up, and started making waffle cones the old-fashioned way— right in the front window for all to see! Customers were thrilled to watch the baking process of the handmade cones. Word spread, and the drive-in survived the tough competition. Doumar's is still open today, baking and serving delicious cones the way Abe Doumar did at the St. Louis World's Fair almost a hundred years ago.

Oh, and the name of the restaurant that almost drove Doumar's out of business? McDonald's!

Oops!

In October of 1954, just six months after the IAICM had proclaimed Ernest Hamwi the creator of the ice cream

---

Historians now believe that glass cones were used by Europeans as early as the 1820s. The French were using paper and metal cones for serving ice cream by the late 1800s. The English were perhaps the first to create edible ice cream dishes. In Agnes B. Marshall's 1894 British cookbook <u>Fancy Ices</u>, she includes recipes for ice-cream-filled pastries. These were called "cornets" because they looked like tiny trumpets. But since proper etiquette required that these fancy desserts be eaten with a spoon and fork, they are not considered true ice cream cones.

cone, the association made a surprising discovery: an Italian immigrant named Italo Marchiony had applied for and received a patent for an ice cream cone machine in 1903—an entire year before the St. Louis World's Fair!

According to Marchiony's grandson, William, his grandfather had worked as a hokeypokey man in the late 1800s, peddling ice cream and lemon ices from a small cart along Wall Street in New York City. He served the frozen treats in "thick-bottomed, oversized whiskey shot glasses." Unfortunately, the glasses often got broken or stolen. And, on the busiest days, Marchiony found it difficult to wash the glasses thoroughly and fast enough to serve his impatient customers. For a while, he tried using paper cones, as he remembered many hokeypokey men had done in Europe. Although people loved the convenience, littering soon became a problem.

Then Marchiony hit on a tasty idea: Why not make an edible holder?

In 1896, the Italian concocted a recipe to make what his grandson would later describe as a "prebaked dough that remained soft enough to be rolled . . . at the time of sale." His customers delighted in these edible packages. Sales increased, and Marchiony was able to buy a fleet of hokeypokey carts, selling his ice-cream-filled containers all over the city.

Seven years later, Marchiony created a machine that looked like an elongated waffle iron that baked ten small pastry cups. He was granted a patent for the Marchiony Mold in September 1903. The cups were so popular that he got rid of his pushcarts and opened a cone-making factory in Hoboken, New Jersey. Later, Marchiony supposedly would make the world's first ice cream sandwich by spreading the dessert between two waffle squares.

Today, the International Ice Cream Association has closed the case of the Mystery of the Ice Cream Cone. Marchiony, they claim, is the true inventor. But is he really? Patent illustrations Marchiony submitted clearly show that his waffle mold made edible cups—not cones. So perhaps Hamwi gets the cone credit after all!

> One third of the ice cream Americans eat each year is scooped into a cone.

One fact remains: the ice cream cone was certainly popularized in 1904 at the St. Louis World's Fair, leading to a highly competitive business. Within two years, catalogs listed cone-making machines that sold for as little as $8.50 apiece. Thousands of one-man ice cream cone vendors opened across the country. Through vendors, ice cream sales soared from fifty million gallons a year in 1904 to eighty million gallons by 1909. More improvements were made in the design of the waffle irons, leading in 1912 to a machine invented by Frederick Bruckman that rolled the cones automatically. Production of the ice cream cone went from one waffle on a hot summer day in 1904 to 245 million cones a year in 1924.

Today, high-tech machines can make 150,000 cones every twenty-four hours. That adds up to 52,800,000 cones a year—from one machine alone!

Anyone for a double-scoop?

> It takes about fifty licks to eat a single-scoop ice cream cone.

Section 3

FOUNTAINS OF YOUTH

At the turn of the twentieth century, the ice cream soda was considered America's national beverage, and children revered and admired the servers—known as "soda jerks"—who concocted these delicious drinks. Although soda jerks were men, one could occasionally find a woman at the fountain pumps, such as this young lady from a small North Dakota town (circa 1900).

Photo credit: Fred Hultstrand History in Pictures Collection,
NDSU, Fargo, North Dakota.

8

Snap, Crackle, and Soda Pop!: Soda Fountains & Soda Jerks

"Eternal vigilance is the price of a good soda. Have an eagle eye . . . never pass the fountain without noting whether the glasses are clean, the fountain and slab immaculate, the holders properly polished, the lemons fresh, the eggs clean, large, and brown—in fact, that everything is in proper shape to tempt a thirsty mortal or to make a mortal thirsty."

—from *How to Make a Soda Fountain Pay*, 1903

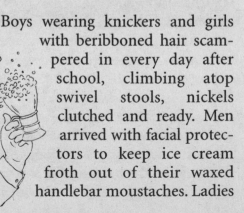

Boys wearing knickers and girls with beribboned hair scampered in every day after school, climbing atop swivel stools, nickels clutched and ready. Men arrived with facial protectors to keep ice cream froth out of their waxed handlebar moustaches. Ladies sipped daintily from frosty glasses, enjoying the cooling breeze of the ceiling fans, and an hour or so unencumbered by escorts.

The Time? Early 1900s. Place? The neighborhood ice cream parlor. The drink? Why, the national beverage, of course: The ice cream soda.

Pop Goes the Water!

The first man-made carbonated water was created in 1767 by Dr. Joseph Priestley of Leeds, England. Sixty-five years later, in 1832, John Matthews created a convenient device for making and dispensing the bubbly liquid in American drugstores. He called his invention the soda fountain.

Doctors and pharmacists had long touted soda water as an aid to digestion and a cure for obesity. The partaking of these plain but allegedly healthy mineral waters soon became a daily habit in the US. One British subject visiting Philadelphia in 1819 remarked that "the first thing every American who can afford five cents . . . takes, on rising in the morning, is a glass of soda water."

In 1838, Eugene Roussel, a French soda water salesman in Philadelphia, got a tasty idea: Why not add a flavoring to the liquid? It would be sweetly delicious and refreshing, and might increase sales even more. Remembering the popularity of the *limonaidiers* in his home country, the Frenchman set about concocting a thick syrup made from water, lemon juice, and sugar. He infused it with the carbonated water and *voilà!* The first soda pop popped onto the scene.

Customers loved the lemon-flavored sodas, and guzzled them by the tumblersful. Within a few years, fountain operators added a wide variety of flavors, such as cherry,

Not long after inventing the world's first soda fountain, John Matthews hired an African-American assistant, Ben Austen, and taught him the soda water trade. Austen had been a slave since birth on a plantation in North Carolina. When his master died, "Old Ben"—as he was called—was freed and traveled north. After his tutelage under Matthews, "Old Ben" became New York City's first soda dispenser, selling the popular drink from a portable fountain on a pushcart. His former mentor, Matthews, eventually would become the world's largest soda fountain manufacturer.

cinnamon, ginger, nectar, nutmeg, peppermint, pineapple, raspberry, root beer, rose, sasparilla, strawberry, vanilla . . . even champagne and celery! An 1863 edition of *The American Dispenser's Book* featured thirteen hundred exotic soda recipes. By the end of the century, customers could order just about any flavor imaginable in the more than sixty thousand soda fountains located across the country.

Our National Beverage

One of the most popular sodas in the mid-nineteenth century was a drink called the ice cream soda. Surprisingly, it contained no ice cream; instead, it was made from sweet cream, flavored syrup, shaved ice, and carbonated water. "People doted on this mixture," read an article in a popular trade journal of that era, "and the man who made the best ice cream soda . . . commanded the best patronage; best both in quality and number."

A soda fountain manufacturer named Robert M.

Green deserves the credit for creating the first soda made with real ice cream. It happened like this:

In October, 1874, Green was running a tiny soda fountain concession stand at Philadelphia's Franklin Institute Exposition. One day, so many customers ordered his cream sodas that Green ran out of the main ingredient. Thinking quickly, he hurried to a pottery booth, where he bought two ceramic pitchers. Then he raced to a confectionary shop, where he purchased enough vanilla ice cream to fill the containers. Green planned to allow the ice cream to melt, substituting it for the sweet cream in his soda recipe. Unfortunately, when he returned to his stand, a line of impatient customers had formed. With no time to lose—or to thaw the dessert—Green plopped scoops of the ice cream into his soda mixture, then stood back anxiously to watch the first drinker.

To his delight, the "result was entirely satisfactory . . ." Green later recalled, "[although] people were slow to try the new novelty. An occasional chance passerby would stop and relish the new food drink, pass on and leave more than enough room for the next comer. But even so, [my] first day's receipts amounted to eight dollars."

Word spread throughout the Exposition, and people flocked to his stand to try the new-and-improved ice cream sodas. By the end of the celebration, Green was earning $400 *a day* hawking the drink. Soon he opened his own fountain-manufacturing business, and placed advertisements for his concoction in newspapers and magazines. One read: "Something new! Green's Ice Cream Soda. The Most Delicious Drink . . . Ten Cents a Glass. Try It and Tell Your Friends!" They did, and soon business was bubbling over at his fountains, which featured innovative flavors such as "chocolate, coffee, coconut, orange, black-

Some sources claim the ice cream soda was invented in 1872 by two unidentified "newsies"—newsboys—who liked to hang out at a confectionary shop in New York City. Much of the money they earned selling papers went for candy. But one day, bored, they asked the fountain dispenser to scoop ice cream and a slice of pineapple into a glass of soda water. Smacking their lips, they next begged for a ginger-ale-and-strawberry concoction, then demanded cold coffee poured over ice cream. "Here, boys," the annoyed fountain owner said at last, "take all the stuff you want, make me a good drink, and it won't cost you a cent." The boys experimented like serious chemists, and the rest is ice cream history . . .

berry, [and] hock," a white German wine.

By 1893, an East Coast newspaper proclaimed the ice cream soda our national beverage. Another newspaper announced: "The ice cream soda is a characteristically American product along with baseball, skyscrapers, hot biscuits . . . Vermont maple sugar . . . rough-riding cowboys, and hooked rugs."

No surprise. The delicious drink was available wherever soda fountains sprang up: drug and department stores, confectionaries and restaurants . . . even hat shops! In New York City alone, there were more soda fountains than bars. Even the smallest of towns had at least one. Since most ice cream establishments were opulent and respectable places to linger—featuring elegant marble countertops, polished mahogany cabinets, gilded mirrors, and flowers galore—they became the main gathering place for people of all ages and means. "Young people do not go for walks in America," wrote one British citizen in the early 1900s. "They chiefly consort in the ice cream parlors." And for good reason. "They are spacious, scrupulously clean, and decorative," another visiting Englishman wrote.

After retiring from his successful fountain business, Green died in 1920, a very wealthy man. An impressive monument erected on his grave reads: *Robert M. Green: Originator of the Ice Cream Soda.* His famous drink would remain America's national beverage for another twenty-five years, and is still a popular menu item.

An unhappy farmer's wife in nineteenth-century Pennsylvania filed for divorce on the grounds that her husband wasted too much of their married life drinking ice cream sodas. Instead of caring for the couple's chickens, the man spent most of their money at the neighborhood soda fountain. The judge sided with the wife, and granted her a divorce. In another case, a Chicago man got in trouble with the law for pulling his wife's hair whenever he drank too much beer. The judge offered the husband a year's probation—if the man switched from drinking alcohol to ice cream sodas!

What a Jerk!

"Don't let the first impression you make be anything but a good one," advised a nineteenth-century soda-fountain manual. "Don't leave your white coat unbuttoned unless you have a white vest on, and don't lean on the counter."

These were just a few recommendations in a seemingly endless list of rules and regulations heaped onto the jerk who manned the fountain—the soda jerk, that is.

Originally called a dispenser or soda clerk, the soda jerk got his nickname because of the short, sharp motion needed when pulling on the draft arms of the fountain pumps. This jerking action drew the fine or coarse squirts and streams of carbonated water needed to make the perfect ice cream soda. (Soda jerks were also sometimes called "The Professor," probably because they looked similar to a mad scientist concocting a mysterious brew.)

Although "jerk" now means a rude or foolish person, the soda jerks of yesteryear were revered and admired. Kids considered them celebrities and role models, and longed to wear a jerk's white cap, apron, necktie, and jacket.

The soda jerks were also looked upon as types of artists and performers, creating and serving ice cream delights with flourish and flair. "Glamorize the mixing and building of your sodas," read a 1940 article in the *Ice Cream Review*. "Your position behind the counter is comparable to being in a show window. You are an artist, demonstrating the right way to mix the perfect chocolate ice cream soda.

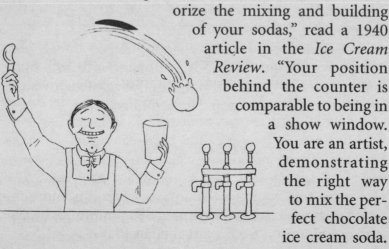

Do it deliberately, carefully, artistically . . ." It was this expertise, talent, and style that was responsible for making the town soda fountain popular and profitable.

"It took me two months just to learn the basics of the profession," recalled Bryce Thomson of Bellevue, Michigan, who became a drugstore soda jerk in 1936. He was handsome, willing to learn, and all of nineteen. "I remember practicing how to throw ice cream balls up in the air between the scoop and the malted can," he said. "You had to be a kind of showman to do it right. I dropped lots of them in private. But I never dropped one in public. I did embarrass myself once, though. I remember putting a malted can onto the mixer, then watching helplessly while it fell off and splattered all over the wall and all over me!"

Thomson—like all soda jerks—had numerous duties. He remembers having to make "all the soda-fountain specialities—not just sodas. Banana splits, floats, malteds, milk shakes, flavored soft drinks. In those days, everything was done by hand. You didn't draw Coke from a dispenser. You made it yourself, using flavored syrup from big wooden barrels and soda water."

A typical day for Thomson started early: 8 A.M. His boss expected him to get the fountain ready, sweep the floors, create window displays and posters, percolate the syrups, wait on customers, fill prescriptions, do the dishes ("all by hand, of course, and the tall soda glasses were hard to clean"), and sell candy, cigars, and gifts. Later, he also created new sodas and ice cream dishes. He was in charge of closing the fountain, too: 6 P.M. on weeknights; 11:30 P.M. on Saturdays. Thomson worked about sixty hours each week, and was earning $80 a month when he hung up his apron for the last time in 1940.

Having to support his mother, two sisters, and a brother during the Great Depression, Thomson felt fortunate to have a job—especially one so "glamorous." Some teens slaved for years pushing brooms or wiping dishes, hoping to work their way up to the coveted counter. Although always exhausted, Thomson enjoyed his four-year stint as a jerk—especially on Saturday nights.

"The drugstore where I worked was the most popular spot in town," he says with a chuckle in his voice, "because it was the *only* spot in town—to hang out, that is. The regulars came in to play pinball or the music box, meet their friends, and guzzle sodas. We watched fights, too, between the farmhands and town toughs. But the best part was when cute teachers would visit with us good lookin' soda jerks. Discouraging, though, when an especially pretty girl would come in. I'd usually get nervous and spill a glass of water in front of her!"

In the 1930s, when Bryce Thomson worked as a soda jerk, the daily newspaper sold for 3 cents, Coke was a nickel, and ice cream sundaes and sodas went for a dime. Malted milks and milk shakes were big-ticket items: a staggering 15 cents apiece.

RULES FOR SODA JERKS
- The finest beverage loses its charm if indifferently served.
- Never refuse anyone a glass of water. A water customer today, a soda customer tomorrow.

- Don't turn your back on a customer. Draw soda water standing sideways.
- Be lavish in every direction—except as to quantity.
- Don't argue with a cranky customer—satisfy him.
- Don't hesitate to change a drink which is not appreciated. And don't keep a customer waiting for a check.
- If you want the best of everything, stand your tumblers with the rims in crushed ice. They will retain their coldness a long time. It pays to study these minor details.
- Women like a little more syrup and three times as much foam and froth as men like. But never overflow the glass. A sloppy soda . . . is unpardonable.

—taken from "How to Make a Chocolate Soda," the *Ice Cream Review*,1940; and the *American Dispenser's Book*, 1863.

The Lickin' Lingo

"A bucket of mud and jerk a bridge through Georgia!"

The customer was perplexed. He'd plunked himself onto the soda fountain stool and given his order: a large scoop of chocolate ice cream and four chocolate sodas. Now it seemed as if the soda jerk was speaking a foreign language. . .

In a way, he was.

On top of all their other amazing skills, soda jerks in the late-nineteenth and early-twentieth centuries developed hundreds of "calls": clever and often amusing terms and phrases for the sodas and ice cream desserts sold in soda fountains. The calls helped jerks remember long and difficult orders, and acted as a shortcut when placing them. Creating the ice cream lingo helped to pass the time when business was slow. The mysterious terms, recognized only by other jerks and cooks, could also warn coworkers that a customer was about to leave without paying a bill, or that a pretty young lady was approaching the counter.

Here are some of the most common calls:

STICK: an ice cream cone
PINK STICK: a strawberry cone (black stick was a chocolate cone; white stick, vanilla)
STRETCH IT: make it a large one
ONE IN: chocolate ice cream soda
ONE IN SHAKE: chocolate milk shake
DROP: sundae
GLOB: plain sundae
HOLD THE HAIL: no ice
MUD: chocolate ice cream
BUCKET: large scoop
BRIDGE: four
THROUGH GEORGIA: add chocolate syrup
95: a customer is leaving without paying
81: glass of plain water (also called Dog Soup, H20, Adam's Ale, and City Juice)
MILK: cow juice
BLACK COW: root beer; sometimes a root beer float
PATCH: strawberry ice cream
VAN: vanilla ice cream
HOUSEBOAT: banana split (also called Split One)
SHAKE: milk shake
IN THE HAY: strawberry milk shake

JERK: Ice Cream Soda
NERVOUS PUDDING: Jell-O
BURN IT AND LET IT SWIM: ice cream float
TWIST IT, CHOKE IT, AND MAKE IT CACKLE:
  chocolate malted milk with egg
ON WHEELS: to go
SALT WATER MAN: the ice cream maker
POP BOY: soda man who doesn't know his business
PEST: assistant manager
SQUIRT: soda jerk
PLAIN VANILLA: Former manager who now works
  behind the counter
87½: a cute girl is coming!
FIZZ: plain carbonated water

The Bubble Bursts

Hotels and cocktail lounges remodeled their smoky bars
into soda fountains. Fountains already in existence
expanded: one on Madison Avenue in New York City featured enough chairs to seat eight hundred people;
another popular fountain in Chicago could serve twelve
hundred customers. Even beer companies got into the act:
breweries, now illegal, were transformed into ice cream
manufacturing plants. A popular song, perfomed to the
tune of "Old Black Joe," sung the praises of Prohibition
and ice cream:

> *Gone are the days when Father was a souse*
> *Gone are the days of the weekly family rows*
> *Gone from this land since prohibition's here—*
> *He brings a brick of ice cream home instead of beer.*

Chorus:
He's coming, he's coming; we can see him coming near—
He brings a brick of ice cream home instead of beer.

As ice cream became even more popular, universities began offering courses in ice-cream-making. Elegant furniture and glassware were designed especially for soda fountains. Soda fountain journals and associations popped up. Movies were made about soda jerks, and the white-coated figure became as recognizable around the world as the American lumberjack or cowboy.

In 1946 the Soda Fountain Manufacturers Association reported there were more than 120,000 soda fountains in the nation. Over a billion and a quarter dollars were earned that year in the business. But by 1947, the bubble had burst—and the soda-fountain industry began to dry up. Historians believe there were several reasons for this. The spread of fast-food restaurants across the country

"Chairs [in a soda fountain] are a good thing," advised the <u>American Soda Book</u> in 1863. "When resting, customers drink slowly. This means looking about and finding other things to buy." Perhaps this observation inspired J. Silverman, a man who built bicycle handlebars. In 1905 he created the classic heart-shaped back chairs by using thick, twisted wire, and sold them to ice cream parlors for $1.25 apiece. Silverman hoped that one day his chairs would become "the most famous furniture in the world." Today, they remain the standard in many ice cream shops, synonymous with the good times and tasty treats of a bygone era.

forced many luncheon-
ettes, diners, and soda
counters to close down;
improvements in me-
chanical refrigeration
meant people could
make and store ice
cream at home; super-
markets and grocery-
store chains found
they could produce the
dessert cheaply, offer-
ing it in bulk at in-
expensive prices; the
invention of TV and
the more widespread

The oldest soda fountain
still in use today is
Goldberg's of Deadwood,
South Dakota, which first
opened it doors in 1876.
The fountain boasts 14
flavor dispensers and 13
swivel stools. The 32-foot-
long counter, made from
a slab of green California
marble, was carted into
town by a team of oxen.

use of cars kept kids and teens at home or on the road—
not twirling on stools at the local fountain.

There are still a few soda fountains scattered across
the country today, dishing up "pink sticks" and "house-
boats" and "Dog Soup—hold the hail!" But most of the
soda jerks have either retired or died. Or they've joined
the National Association of Soda Jerks where they can
meet, swap old soda recipes, and serve up scoops of delicious nostalgia.

9

Monday through Sundae:
The Invention of the Ice Cream Sundae and the Banana Split

Little Boy Blue, go blow your horn,
There's ice cream aplenty as sure as you're born;
Go call in the children—I want them to share
In our wonderful luncheon of rich, frozen fare.

—The *Soda Fountain Magazine*, May 1915

The chorus of the 1927 hit "(I Scream—You Scream—We All Scream for) Ice Cream" cheered on Tuesdays and Mondays for . . . sundaes. No surprise. Since the 1880s, the ice cream sundae, in over a hundred variations, had been the second most popular item on soda-fountain menus all over the country. "I'm sorry it is," complained the manager of a New York parlor, "for a sundae requires so much time for service and cleansing the dishes and spoons afterward. But the public must get what it wants."

And want it they did. In fact, it was the insistence of a teenager that started the craze for this new frozen dessert . . . a dessert that would one day become another American institution.

A Cool Idea

Kids in Two Rivers, Wisconsin, loved to hang out at Ed Berners's ice cream parlor. A bowl of vanilla ice cream sold for only a nickel, and Berners dished up a ton of them every day. But one night in 1881, a teen named George Hallauer had a hankering for something different.

As Berners's scoop was poised to fill Hallauer's ice cream order, the teen pointed to a bottle on the back bar.

"Put some of that stuff on the ice cream," he said.

Berners thought the kid was crazy. "Do you want to ruin the ice cream flavor?" he asked, incredulous. "That's used in making sodas!"

Hallauer shrugged. "I'll try anything once," he replied.

Berners shrugged, too, and poured a swirl of chocolate syrup onto the ice cream. Hallauer ate it . . . liked it . . . and ordered another bowl!

Soon, other kids in the shop wanted to try the new dish. As its popularity increased, Berners experimented with spooning an array of syrups and toppings—crushed fruit, marshmallows, even puffed rice!—over the concoction. He called his experiments Flora Dora, Mudscow, and the Jennie Flip. No one flipped over the names. Most customers simply asked for ice cream with "stuff on it."

Word of the nameless treat spread six miles away to George Giffy's ice cream parlor in Manitowoc, Wisconsin. Giffy's was another popular hangout for teens. Soon his customers were requesting ice cream with chocolate sauce, too. Giffy thought they were crazy, and refused to fill the orders. But the kids kept insisting.

Clueless and curious, Giffy drove his wagon down the bumpy road to Berners's store. He stormed into the parlor and confronted the owner. Why was Berners serving something so ridiculous? "It will put us all out of business at a nickel a dish!" he shouted.

Wordlessly, Berners set a bowl in front of him. Giffy spooned up the dessert in a hurry, and his "ridiculous!" changed to "delicious!" That afternoon, he and Berners decided they could afford to sell the luscious treat if they featured it only on Sundays.

Not long after, a little girl came into Giffy's parlor on a weekday. Nickel clutched tightly in her fist, she ordered the popular "ice cream with stuff on it."

"I serve that only on Sundays," Giffy apologized.

"Then it must be Sunday," replied the tot, "for that's the kind of ice cream I want!"

Giffy gave in, the girl got her wish, and the dessert finally got a name: The Ice Cream Sunday.

According to the International Ice Cream Association, more ice cream is sold on Sunday than on any other day of the week.

Sundae Is Fundae

No one knows for sure when the "y" in Sunday was replaced by an "e." Many historians believe it began because of city ordinances called Blue Laws. Toward the beginning of the twentieth century, Blue Laws in the Southern states and on the East Coast forbade people from dancing, playing games, going to shows or sports events, and running their businesses on Sunday. One soda fountain operator in Pennsylvania was actually arrested for selling ice cream on the Sabbath! The case went to a jury trial, but the operator was acquitted. His defense: Since many doctors at that time prescribed the wholesome, calcium-laden treat for their patients, ice cream was actually a medicine, not a dessert!

Religious groups were especially aghast at the thought of its young people "sucking soda"—especially when sinful couples shared the same glass. They believed that hanging out at the local soda fountain was a bad influence on teenagers, and youngsters needed to spend their Sundays at home, taking part in more holy pastimes, such as meditation and prayer. So the sale of ice cream sodas on Sunday afternoons was banned in many small towns across the country.

Historians from Evanston, Illinois, believe the ice cream sundae originated there in the 1880s at a drugstore/soda fountain owned by William C. Garwood. (Garwood's store was also the home of the first carhop, offering "curbside" service to customers who arrived in carriages and wagons.) Soda jerks in this particularly strict town were the first to fight back against what the pious called the "Sunday Soda Menace." When forbidden to make their popular ice cream sodas, they simply tossed out the seltzer water, and poured syrups over a dish of ice cream instead. The "Sodaless Soda" was a hit, and soon became known as a Sunday. To keep from getting a sacriligeous reputation and further infuriating religious groups, soda jerks quickly changed the spelling to sun*dae*. And sundae it has remained, seven days a week, for more than a hundred years.

Let's split!

The "Flaming Nut Sundae" was banned in the 1920s as a fire hazard by city officials in Pittsfield, Massachusetts. The recipe called for a small sugar cube to be dipped in lemon extract, placed on top of the sundae, and lit afire. Since lemon extract has an alcohol content of 70 percent, the dessert was considered highly flammable and dangerous to soda-fountain patrons.

The banana split is nothing more than an ice cream sundae gone . . . bananas. Served for the first time to the National Association of Retail Druggists at their Boston convention in 1906 (just fourteen years after the US began to import the fruit), the NARD raved, saying that among all the treats served there, ". . . none was more novel with the ladies than the banana split."

Yet the novelty didn't wear off. A Boston soda jerk named Stinson Thomas had begun serving splits at his fountain in 1905, using only a dozen bananas a day. "If [they] were not used up . . . I instructed my dispensers to prepare banana splits and *give* them away," he later recalled. A year later, Thomas was going through five bunches of bananas a day to prepare the most popular item on his menu. Customers came from miles around to taste the treat. "In the busy hours," Thomas said, "I am able to do little else beside splitting bananas for dispensers."

People first went bananas over banana splits in 1904 in Latrobe, Pennsylvania. David Strickler, a young soda jerk who wanted to train as a pharmacist, took a job at a drugstore there. "He was always a great experimenter," his daughter, Nancy, remembered, and soon created a ten-cent sensation: a dish made with three scoops of ice cream on a halved banana. (The banana was not peeled first.) Strickler then ladled more goodies onto the dessert: chocolate syrup, marshmallows, nuts, whipped cream, and a cherry.

Enough toppings for sundaes and splits are sold every year to cover 390 million servings of ice cream.

The concoction was huge, so there were no dishes big enough to hold it. That didn't faze Strickler. He sketched a dish of his own and had a local glass company design and produce it. Today, the banana is the unofficial mascot for Latrobe. The local college retells the banana-split story in pamphlets about the school, hosts "Banana Split Bashes," and sells banana T-shirts in its campus bookstore.

And, of course, you can still indulge in a banana split, just as in the olden days, at Strickler's drugstore.

According to the Guinness Book of World Records, the largest banana split in the world was made on April 30, 1988, by the residents of Selinsgrove, Pennsylvania. The split stretched a total of 4.5 miles. Employees of Palm Dairies, Ltd. of Edmonton, Alberta, Canada, dished up the world's largest ice cream sundae on July 24, 1988. It consisted of 44,689 pounds of ice cream, 9,688 pounds of chocolate syrup, and 537 pounds of toppings.

Section 4

WHAT AN IDEA!: Ice Cream Novelties

The neighborhood Good Humor Man—with his crisp, white uniform, friendly smile, and a truck filled with frozen ice cream treats—became the Pied Piper of the 1940s and 1950s.

Photo credit: Courtesy Good Humor–Breyers

• 10 •

Pie in the Sky:
The Story Behind the
Eskimo Pie

There's no bother for mother
It's good for father and brother
NEW ESKIMO PIE
CREAM-Y PIE ON A STICK
Little Billy and Mable
Eat it all but the Label
And they're sorry they can't eat the stick.

—from the song "New Eskimo Pie on a Stick"
by Dale Wimbrow, 1941

Take one young teacher who taught psychology, the science of the mind.

Add one young, freckle-faced boy, who couldn't *make up* his mind.

Mix both ingredients briefly on a spring morning in 1920. Bake for several months to create a recipe for super success: a new dessert dubbed the I-Scream-Bar.

Within two years, one million I-Scream-Bars would be selling *every day*. People would call their creator the Thomas Edison of the dairy industry, and the dessert would undergo a radical name change. Soon manufacturers all over the country would be I-screaming for their own piece of the pie—Eskimo Pie, that is: the world's first chocolate-covered ice cream treat.

Ice Cream Dream

Christian K. Nelson, the main ingredient in this delicious recipe, was born in Denmark to a dairyman and his wife in 1893. Soon after, the family moved to America. Over the years, they lived in several states in their adopted country, finally settling down, when Chris was nine, in Moorehead, Iowa. There, Mr. Nelson worked in a creamery, making butter and cheese.

By 1908, the family had saved enough money to start its own creamery. Every day, fifteen-year-old Chris and his brother, Nels, drove a horse-drawn wagon to the countryside, picking up milk from farmers and delivering it to their father's business. The milk was made into a variety of dairy products, including—at Chris's urging—ice cream.

In those days, few people manufactured and sold ice cream commercially in that part of the country. Families either made it themselves or did without. Or they paid high prices to have it brought in by train for special occasions. Chris believed that his father could make a good living if he expanded the creamery to include a small ice cream factory. His instincts proved correct: The family sold ten thousand gallons its first year in business. Mr. Nelson used the profits to take his wife and seven children back to Denmark to visit their grandmother. He had enough money left over to send Chris to the University of Nebraska, where the teen studied to become a teacher.

After graduating in 1916, Chris worked as a high-school principal for two years until Uncle Sam called. America had entered World War I in 1917, and almost every healthy young man was needed now to fight overseas. During the tough months of war, Chris often thought about his father's success in the ice cream business. Although he had enjoyed working with students, he had plans to make ice cream his life, too. As soon as the war ended, he packed away his boots and canteen and marched off to the small town of Onawa, Iowa, to open an ice cream parlor. He chose a site near the local school. There, he figured, he'd never want for customers.

Chris figured wrong.

To his great disappointment, sales were slow. They slowed even more during the cooler months. People still considered ice cream a seasonal food, rarely eating it in fall and winter.

When summer ended in 1919, Chris sadly realized he could no longer afford to keep the parlor running full-time. That September, he took a position teaching Latin, math, and psychology at Onawa High School. But he couldn't completely give up his ice cream dream. He hurried to the shop early every morning, selling candy, gum, sodas, and ice cream to the kids for an hour or so before classes began. Then, after a long day of teaching, he rushed back to the shop in time to scoop up more treats for the small afternoon and evening crowds.

Decisions, Decisions

On a warm spring morning in 1920, a young boy named Douglass Fessenden stopped into Nelson's shop on the way to school. He was late for class, but just *had* to buy a candy bar. He plunked some change on the counter, and asked for his favorite brand.

"Sold out," Nelson told him. Would he like to choose another?

Douglass hemmed and hawed, then pointed. Nelson reached into the display case.

"Um, I've changed my mind," Douglass announced. "I'd rather have an ice cream sandwich."

Nelson nodded, and made his way across the parlor to the soda fountain. He sliced a slab of vanilla ice cream and picked up two cookie wafers. He was just about to smush them together, when . . .

"Mr. Nelson," Douglass called. "I've changed my mind again. May I have this mallow-nut bar instead?"

Ever patient, the teacher sold him the candy bar without complaint. Content at last, Douglass raced off to class. But long after the boy had disappeared, Nelson was still mulling the incident over in his mind.

Why had Douglass chosen the candy bar instead of the ice cream sandwich?

Then, in a flash, the answer hit him.

Chocolate. The boy had a craving for something chocolaty! Douglass might've ordered an ice cream sundae with rich fudge sauce, but he was late for school and didn't have time to eat it. So the candy bar had won out.

Then, as Nelson locked up his shop—another flash!

Would it be possible to freeze a coating of chocolate around a slice of ice cream? The concoction sounded simple, easy, and delicious. Nelson rushed to school. The sooner he got there, the sooner the day would be over. He couldn't wait to get back to his shop and begin experimenting!

The Crazy Professor

Nelson spent most of that afternoon and evening in the back room of his shop. He pulled out pots and pans and bags of ingredients. Then he whipped up a bowl of chocolate cake frosting, and dipped a slab of vanilla ice cream into the mixture.

Too thick. The chocolate slipped right off.

Next he tried thinning the frosting with milk and water. But the chocolate still wouldn't stick to the ice cream.

Finally, Nelson heated the frosting on a hot plate to make it smooth and liquidy. Once again, he dipped a slice of ice cream into the mixture. Then he plunged the bar into his "refrigerator"—a wooden tub full of ice and salt—to chill it. But the cold chest couldn't cool the ice cream fast enough. It melted into a mushy mess. Even worse, the chocolate turned icy and inedible.

Nelson went home that night disappointed, but not discouraged. He vowed to continue his experiments until he got the recipe right.

Soon, the whole town knew that Nelson was trying to invent something. Only a few hundred people lived in Onawa, so gossip was a favorite pastime. Whispers turned to catcalls. Teasing turned to taunts. Kids would snicker and holler out "Hello, inventor!" whenever they saw the shy man outside his shop. Even the old-timers who sat in rocking chairs along the storefronts on Main Street thought him foolish. Everyone knew you couldn't make hot chocolate stick to ice cream, they murmured. Why, Chris Nelson must be crazy!

Nelson did his best to ignore the jokes and jibes. But after weeks of failed experiments, he, too, began to have doubts. Cake frosting didn't work. Neither did melted chunks of chocolate. Nothing would stick to the ice cream. Nothing. The inventor grew depressed.

Then, one day, he struck up a conversation with a candy salesman who had come into the ice cream shop. As the salesman restocked the empty shelves with fresh confections, Nelson said, "Say, what do the candy companies put in the chocolate coatings of their candy bars?"

Chocolate, of course, the salesman answered. Oh, and sugar, milk solids, and cocoa butter.

Cocoa butter? Nelson had never heard of such an ingredient.

The salesman explained that cocoa butter was a yellowish white fat extracted from the cacao bean—the same bean from which chocolate was made. Candy manufacturers used the butter to make the thick, melted chocolate more liquid, yet sticky. That way, the sugars and milk solids would mix and hold together in a formed bar.

Nelson could feel his enthusiasm growing again. Maybe cocoa butter was the answer! He scraped together enough money to purchase a ten-pound slab from the salesman. Then he burned the midnight oil for several weeks. Like a mad scientist, he mixed his precious ingredients, heated them on the stove, then dunked the ice cream into the chocolate soup, freezing it immediately in his icy, wooden tub.

Melt, dip, chill. Melt, dip, chill.

The chocolate coating, when frozen, continued to fall off the vanilla ice cream. But Nelson did not give up.

Melt, dip, chill.

Nelson measured and mixed, experimenting with different formulas and temperatures, until one night the chocolate grew sticky, stickier, stickiest . . .

. . . and stuck fast and hard to the ice cream!

Nelson took a nibble. Then a bite. Then he gobbled the entire bar. Delicious! It was the fall of 1920. After six months of late and lonely nights, Chris Nelson had created the most innovative frozen dessert since the ice cream cone.

The I-Scream Bar

The next morning, Nelson hopped the first train out of town and headed to Omaha, Nebraska, the nearest large city. There, he hired a lawyer, and the two of them sat down to draw up and submit a petition for a patent. Nelson knew that his invention would be a taste sensation, and wanted to protect his legal rights to what he called the I-Scream-Bar.

Upon his return, Nelson started selling the I-Scream-Bar in his shop. It was an instant hit with kids and adults alike. Townsfolk, who just a few days before had teased him mercilessly about the hopelessness of his experiments, now gobbled his invention and urged him to go national. But expanding his business would take money, and Nelson had very little. He first approached his landlord, then a local banker, about a loan. Both turned him down, believing the I-Scream-Bar was just a flash-in-the-scoop that only the locals could love.

Then a friend of Nelson's in Omaha suggested that he make an appointment with the owner of the Graham Ice Cream Company. The friend knew that the company made both ice cream and candy. Perhaps with those experiences in mind, Mr. Graham might offer the financial backing the I-Scream-Bar so desperately needed. Nelson agreed to give it a shot and stopped in at the factory. A secretary told him that Mr. Graham had traveled out-of-town. Would he be willing to meet with the candy superintendent instead? Nelson agreed and was ushered into the office of Russell Stover.

"I'm convinced that the I-Scream-Bar has tremendous potential," Nelson told him. "Ice cream cones sell at the rate of ten million a day, six months of the year. Hershey bars sell at the rate of eight million a day. My invention is a unique combination of ice cream and chocolate candy. It's bound to have universal appeal."

Stover wholeheartedly agreed. He whisked out a piece of paper, and on Graham Ice Cream Co. stationery, hastily handwrote an agreement to form a partnership. Stover would provide the money needed to start the company, and would act as manager. The two young men would share any profits earned from that day forward. The date was July 13, 1921.

A Memorable Moniker

The first order of business, Russell Stover decided, was a fancy, catchy name. That very afternoon, Stover left his job at the Graham Ice Cream Co. He, his sister, and Nelson hurried to the Omaha Public Library. There, they spent hours riffling through dictionaries and thesauruses, jotting down words and phrases that conjured up images of cold. They collected several hundred. With scribbled list in hand, they continued brainstorming that night around the dinner table. They asked five other people to help them: Stover's wife; his brother-in-law; Mrs. Stover's sister and brother-in-law; and the foreman from the candy department at the Graham Ice Cream Company.

As the night wore on, the group narrowed their ideas down to two: Eskimo and Icy-ette. Mrs. Stover pushed for the latter. Her husband almost agreed—the hour was late, everyone was exhausted and wanted to go home. Still, Icy-ette didn't wow them. And if not them, it might not impress the American public, either.

Then Stover remembered the brand of a popular new candy bar: Kandy Kake. Stover believed part of the bar's success was due to its clever name. For the first time in history, a household dessert—cake—had been used in the marketing of a candy.

Perhaps, suggested Stover, the I-Scream-Bar should carry a moniker featuring another household dessert, such as pie.

"Eskimo Pie!" Nelson shouted.

"That's it!" Stover cheered. The vote was unanimous, and plans to market Eskimo Pies nationally began the very next day.

"It's Coming"

In the fall of 1921, delivery trucks for the Hutcheson Ice Cream Company drove through the streets of Des Moines, Iowa, carrying signs with those two simple words.

A few days later, the signs were changed to read "?"

The following week, the signs, written in exuberant

script, announced: "It's here! ESKIMO PIE!"

The teasing advertising campaign worked. Within two days, crowds of people lined up at ice cream shops all over town to buy the new frozen treat wrapped in the gleaming foil wrapper. And the word continued to spread. Not only did people want to eat the dessert, but ice cream manufacturers wanted the opportunity to make and sell it. Nelson and Stover were bombarded with telegrams, letters, and phone calls, *begging* for information on how to get a financial piece of the Pie. Their makeshift, temporary office in a hotel room was soon filled with customers who spilled out the door and down the hallway. At last the hotel management grew weary of the noise and confusion. Nelson and Stover were asked to leave.

After setting up a new office, the partners decided their business would work best if they sold franchises of Eskimo Pie. This meant that for about $1,000, ice cream manufacturers could purchase the recipe and the right to make the confection. They would also pay Nelson and Stover 10 cents for every dozen Pies sold.

And sell they did. Over the next four months, twenty-seven hundred companies plunked down substantial chunks of change to become franchises. Two months later, in the spring of 1922, one million Eskimo Pies were selling across the country *every day*. By early summer that figure had risen to two million.

Nelson became an overnight sensation, his picture and rags-to-riches story plastered all over the pages of every major newspaper. The roaring twenties song "(I Scream You Scream—We all Scream for) Ice Cream" became a hit, featuring a story about a make-believe arctic college called Oo-gie-wa-wa with a cheerleader whose face was frozen "like an ESKIMO Pie."

R.S. Reynolds, known as the Aluminum Foil King and owner of the United States Foil Company, contracted with Stover and Nelson to manufacture the wrappers for Eskimo Pie. To meet the high demand, his plant ran twenty-four hours a day, seven days a week, cranking out five hundred million wrappers in the first six months of production. He sold the wrappers for $4 per thousand—earning $2 free and clear on each batch. When he met Nelson soon after, he pumped the inventor's hand, and boasted, "Young man, I've just made a million dollars on your idea!"

Kids, of course, became big cheerleaders of the 5-cent dessert. So did ice-cream-parlor and soda-fountain owners. Just one year before, they had been suffering through the economic depression of 1921. Because of Eskimo Pie, ice cream would no longer be a seasonal food, and these same companies could now make a profit on ice cream sales year round.

Struggling businesses in South America, Switzerland, and Holland let out a rah-rah-rah, too. After bordering on financial ruin during the depression, cacao-bean growers and chocolate makers were now in great demand. Orders for their products and services poured in from the United States. The people of Ecuador were so grateful, they sent an "official delegation to [the US] to express heartfelt thanks to Chris Nelson for saving their country from bankruptcy."

Trouble in Paradise

"Polar Cake." "Arctic Snow." "Sundae-ette."

These and hundreds of other copycat frozen desserts had snowballed their way into the market by 1923. Although Nelson had received a patent for his invention the year before, the imitators didn't care, blatantly stealing his idea and reaping the resulting profits. (According to the US Patent Office, they sold hundreds of thousands of copies of Nelson's patent—more than any other patent in history.) There was no way Nelson could afford to track down and sue every patent violator. Soon, because of the expensive lawsuits, and other financial and managerial problems, the company was in debt to the tune of $100,000. Everyone was making money off Nelson's invention—everyone except Nelson himself.

Russell Stover decided enough was enough. He sold his half of the business to Nelson and opened a company in Denver, Colorado, creating and selling Mrs. Stover's Bungalow Candies—a soon-to-be-famous chocolate candy company. Nelson and a new partner restructured the firm, opening the Eskimo Pie Corporation. A year later, still struggling under the weight of financial problems, they sold the corporation to the United States Foil Company (now called Reynolds Metals Company) for $40,000.

As part of the deal, Nelson went to work in the technical department of the company. There, in 1924, he invented a machine that resembled a small windmill that could cut "a two-gallon slab [of vanilla ice cream] into bars and automatically dip them." (Eskimos Pies, up until that time, had always been hand-dipped, a slow and painstaking process.)

Nelson also designed a special shipping package for Eskimo Pies made of balsa wood. With the help of a new invention called dry ice, the package could keep ten dozen Eskimo Pies hard as bricks for more than a month. (Dry ice is made from carbon dioxide, a gas which when compressed hardens into solid, snowlike cakes. The temperature of dry ice is so cold—negative 78.5 degrees Celsius—that if touched without special gloves it can cause serious burns.)

The success of Nelson's shipping boxes helped to make the inventors of dry ice rich. It also revolutionized the dairy and shipping industries. Now, frozen or perishable foods such as butter, cottage cheese, milk, sour cream, and ice cream could be shipped cheaply without fear of a meltdown or spoilage. Nelson's ingenious idea had also opened the doors for the development, distribution, and advertising of national product brands.

But Nelson was just warming up in his quest for cold. Next, he designed a thermos in the shape of a large jug in which two dozen Eskimo Pies could be stored and displayed. With a chunk of dry ice inside, the jugs stayed cold all day on the counters at gas stations, grocery stores, cigar shops, news and candy stands, and in soda fountains— right in plain view for all the customers to see. This helped to increase impulse sales: meaning, people who hadn't thought about buying an Eskimo Pie when they

In the 1920s, the Dry Ice Corporation of America sold a hundred thousand pounds of dry ice every day to the Eskimo Pie factory in Brooklyn, New York.

walked into the store did so after seeing the clever display jug which boasted the slogan: "Eskimo Pie—real ice cream enrobed in chocolate." Sales increased so dramatically that the jugs often had to be refilled several times a day. In New York City alone, two hundred deliverymen were needed to replenish the containers with fresh Eskimo Pies.

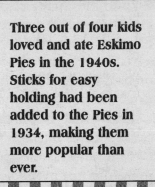

Three out of four kids loved and ate Eskimo Pies in the 1940s. Sticks for easy holding had been added to the Pies in 1934, making them more popular than ever.

A New Challenge

With lifelong royalties guaranteed, Nelson decided to retire in 1928 at the young age of thirty-five. He and his wife, Myrtle, moved to Los Angeles, where they lived and raised four orphan boys.

But Nelson's quick, sharp mind couldn't remain idle for long. He was coaxed back to work at the Eskimo Pie Corporation in 1935. For the next twenty-seven years, he wore a number of hats at the firm, including business promoter, product developer, researcher, engineer and— his favorite—inventor.

For many years, Eskimo Pies had been made using the same, slow process. Soft, almost liquid ice cream was poured into bar-shaped molds, then the molds were plunged into salt water that had been chilled to 35–40 degrees below zero. As soon as the ice cream froze, the molds were removed from the brine and dunked into hot water. This loosened the ice cream enough that it could be removed, coated in chocolate, and packaged. Although certainly much faster than the hand-dipped method, the mold-and-brine system required a lot of manpower and hours.

In 1947, Louis Reynolds, who had taken his father's place as head of the famous aluminum company, came to Nelson with an idea. Perhaps the inventor could create a machine that would squeeze out ice cream like toothpaste from a tube. Called the extrusion method, it was used all the time with hot, liquid aluminum. Why not with ice cream, too?

Nelson accepted the challenge. It took four years, but he finished the first experimental model in 1951. The mechanism successfully pushed out long, continuous snakes of ice cream, then cut them into the Eskimo-Pie-sized bars—seventy-two hundred an hour! He received several patents for the Eskimo Machine in 1955, and the company's franchisees still use variations of it today.

Although Nelson retired a second time from the Eskimo Pie Corporation in 1962, he continued to tinker and toy with ideas for another thirty years. "Each time I visited Chris," said David Clark, the corporation's president, "he had a new invention in his kitchen, like ice cream that wouldn't melt. Chris was a pioneer and an entrepreneur who had a great vision . . ."

It was that vision, combined with intelligence, perseverance, and passion, that helped make Eskimo Pie—and

---

You would need a tower of 1,209 Eskimo Pies, stacked end to end, to stand as high as the Washington Monument. It would take a chain of three billion Eskimo Pies to reach the moon.

the frozen novelty market—an American institution. Eskimo Pie Corporation products are stocked in 95 percent of all grocery stores, and the Pies themselves still sell over one million a day—an amazing figure, especially since there are five hundred brands and two thousand frozen novelty products currently available. You can treat your taste buds while traveling, too, munching Eskimo Pies in faraway places such as Russia, Singapore, Australia, Guam, the Philippines, Puerto Rico, Cuba, Panama, Mexico, England, Canada, and Luxembourg, to name just a few.

> The world's largest ice cream bar was made by the staff of Augusto, Ltd., in Kalisz, Poland, in September, 1994. It weighed 19,357 pounds.

Christian K. Nelson died in Laguna Hills, California, on March 8, 1992—just four days before his ninety-ninth birthday. But his delicious ice cream confection lives on. As the song says:

> *All the girls are now eating*
> *All the boys are now treating*
> *NEW ESKIMO PIE*
> *CREAM-Y PIE ON A STICK.*
> *Go in any direction*
> *You can buy this confection*
> *NEW ESKIMO PIE ON A STICK.*

• 11 •

The Good Humor Man

When the jingling sings
On the street next to yours,
When you stop and you freeze
To make sure that you heard,
Move your knees!
Get your shoes!
Find some coins!
Spread the news!
If you want a sweet lick
Then you've got to be quick!
Skip your chores!
On your feet!
Out the door!
Down the street!
Go so fast you take wing!
Can you feel
The appeal
Of this bell-tinkling thing . . .
This Pied Piper on wheels?

—"Pied Piper" by April Halprin Wayland

He was "better known than the fire chief, more welcome
than the mailman, more respected than the corner cop,"

claimed *Time* magazine. He earned the reputation for rushing expectant mamas to the hospital ... rescuing children from burning homes ... foiling gangsters ... and always having a crisp salute or a tip of the hat for passersby. Children loved him. *Dogs* loved him. From coast-to-coast his immaculate uniform became a symbol of goodness, good times, and America.

Who was this famous hero?

Superman? Hercules? Arnold Schwarzenegger?

None other than your friendly, neighborhood ice cream salesman: the Good Humor Man.

Jolly Good!

School's out!

When the final bell rang and books were put away for the day, you could always find the children of Youngstown, Ohio, in the candy shop of Harry B. Burt. Lollipops were popular in 1910, and the locals especially loved Burt's own creation: the Jolly Boy Sucker. Since many people at that time believed good food could help create a good mood, Burt soon changed the confection's name to the Good Humor Sucker.

The sucker was a sweet success for more than a decade. Such a success that when Eskimo Pies gained frosty fame in the 1920s, Burt tinkered with the idea of inventing another taste treat. Perhaps he, too, could combine his knowledge of both the candy and frozen-dessert industry to create a chocolate-covered ice cream bar.

As a sideline, Burt had for years made batches of ice cream in the basement of his candy store. His son, Harry Burt Jr. worked for him there every day, hand-cranking the ice cream freezer. Now the two of them began to experiment. Late one night, they concocted a recipe using cocoa butter and coconut oil to help their chocolate coating adhere to the vanilla ice cream. It worked! Harry Sr. gave the first bar they made to his daughter, Ruth, for an official taste test.

Delicious! she exclaimed. Only one problem: the mess.

Burt had to agree. As it melted, the bar left a sticky, drippy goo all over Ruth's fingers and face.

Back to the basement—and the drawing board.

As the night wore on, Ruth's brother hit on a clever solution. They had boxes full of wooden sticks stored in the shop for making the Good Humor Sucker. Why not put these same handles on the ice cream bars, creating a frozen lollipop?

Burt Sr. found the idea appealing. Not only would a handle make the "sucker" easier and neater to eat, but it would be more sanitary, too.

The Burts set to work. They began by softening the ice cream just enough to insert a stick into one end. Then they dipped the bar into their mixture of melted chocolate. They packed the bars in brine, or salt water, to harden them again, and the sticks stuck! When chilled, the mois-

Harry Burt Sr. applied for patents for both the machine and process for making Good Humor Bars in January 1922. Urban lore tells that Burt had to wait three years before receiving approval, although records show the patents were granted in October of 1923. Supposedly, the applications got tied up in bureaucratic red tape, and were approved only after Burt Jr. visited the Washington, DC, patent office in person. He took with him a five-gallon jug stacked with Good Humor Bars, and insisted the officials eat them then and there. They did—and the petitions were granted at once.

ture in the handles created miniscule ice crystals that helped the ice cream cling to the wood.

It was 3 A.M. Despite the late hour, the Burts boxed the dessert in dry ice, grabbed their hats, and hurried out into the cold. They were determined to find a notary public who could start the snowball rolling for a patent. Burt Sr. called his new invention the Good Humor Ice Cream Sucker— later known as the Good Humor Bar—the world's first ice cream lollipop!

Two Dairy Queen franchise owners created a yummy chocolate-dipped soft-serve dessert on a stick in 1955, calling it the Dilly bar. Dairy Queen sold so many of the treats that their distributors couldn't keep up with the stick orders. Dairy Queen hit on a healthy alternative: they bought wooden tongue depressors from medical supply houses!

Jingle Bells, Jingle Bells

A unique product deserved a unique sales plan, Harry Burt Sr. decided. Why wait for customers to come to him when he could go to the customers? He repainted his old candy-store delivery truck bright white, and decorated it with the bells from the family sleigh. He loaded the bay with seven hundred pounds of ice and salt, and hundreds of Good Humor Bars. Then he and Burt Jr. drove up and down the neighborhood streets of Youngstown, the tinkling bells announcing their arrival around every corner.

Curious children poured into the streets. They followed the truck as if it were the Pied Piper of Hamelin. Before long, the jingle of bells turned into the jangle of coins as nickels and dimes were traded for the new ice cream treat. Within a few months, Burt needed twelve delivery trucks to meet demand. Each truck was driven by a specially trained "Good Humor Man," who always wore a crisp, white uniform and a friendly smile.

The unique sales plan had worked. Now the Burts could expand their territory to include large cities such as Detroit, Michigan, and Miami, Florida. Unfortunately, Harry Burt Sr. did not live to see how famous his invention would become. He died in 1926, only three years after receiving his patent for the Good Humor Ice Cream Sucker.

An Offer He Could Refuse

After the death of Burt Sr. the family decided to sell its Good Humor patents. Several businessmen from Cleveland, Ohio, shelled out for the whole shebang, starting a company called the Good Humor Corporation of America. The company worked much like the Eskimo Pie Corporation. Franchises were sold to ice cream men around the country, who for a small down payment of $100 bought the right to sell Good Humor products. (Harry Burt Jr. bought one of the franchises from the corporation, opening Burt's Good Humor Ice Cream Company in Tulsa, Oklahoma, in 1928.)

One of the first new franchise owners was a man from Tennessee named Tom Brimer. He sold Good Humor in Detroit, and soon earned enough money to open another franchise in Chicago, Illinois.

Not long after Brimer set up operations there, the Mob paid him a "social call." In the 1920s and '30s, the underworld—groups of gangsters and other violent criminals—terrorized the people of Chicago, especially small-business owners. If protection money wasn't paid, the gangsters threatened murder and mayhem. The Mob demanded that Brimer pay them an exorbitant amount from his Good Humor profits (some sources say they demanded $5,000!)—otherwise, they would blow up his trucks. Brimer refused. Then he contacted his insurance agent, buying more property insurance—just in case.

Smart move. Within days, the gangsters had followed through on their threat. Eight of Brimer's Good Humor trucks were blown to pieces.

The bombing backfired on the underworld. Shock waves roiled across the country. Newspapers in every major city carried the story with indignant front-page headlines. This gave Good Humor—and Brimer's stand against the Mob—free publicity. Not only did sales increase dramatically for the Good Humor men, so did their reputation. From then on, they would become a symbol for honesty and decency in America.

Despite the stock market crash of 1929 and the Great Depression that followed, the Good Humor Corporation continued to grow. Candy, gum, and ice cream were the only luxuries most Americans could afford, so companies that manufactured these products did fairly well even in the leanest of times. By 1941, Good Humor production plants had opened in three major cities, with franchises in New York, Pennsylvania, New Jersey, California, and 12 other states. Soon, fleets of Good Humor trucks, tricycles, and pushcarts rumbled through urban streets all across the US, dishing up tunes and ice cream treats for millions of children.

Another famous frozen "lollipop" was invented in 1905 by an eleven-year-old boy named Frank Epperson. One winter evening in Oakland, California, Frank mixed a packet of powdered soda pop and water in a glass on his back porch. He stirred it with a wooden stick – then went to bed, completely forgetting about his drink. Temperatures dipped to freezing that night. When Frank awoke the next morning, he found his pop had transformed into a delicious, sweet icicle on a stick. He named the accidental invention after himself, calling it the Epperson Icicle, or Epsicle, for short. Some sources claim he froze batch after batch of the "Epsicles" in the family icebox the following summer, selling them to his neighborhood friends for five cents each. In 1924, at the age of thirty, Frank finally patented his creation—which is now famous around the world. You know it today as the Popsicle!

Making Good with Good Humor

"*Delicious,*" Ruth Burt had exclaimed, describing her father's invention. And customers everywhere agreed. But it wasn't the ice cream dessert so much as the Good Humor men who sold it that brought the company national fame.

Before beginning work, each new driver received several weeks of intensive training, along with a handbook called *Making Good with Good Humor.* The rules at Good Humor were strict but logical. To provide excellent service, and to help guarantee repeat customers, the image and quality of Good Humor's salesmen needed to be as high as the quality of its ice cream. Here are just a few examples of what the drivers were taught:

Personal Hygiene

All Good Humor men were "expected to maintain the highest standards of personal hygiene." This meant clean hands, a shaved face, trimmed fingernails, and frequent haircuts. "Body odor, unclean teeth, bad breath, and the like are, of course, inexcusable," read the handbook. Oh, and "change your socks every day." (Does this sound like your mother?!)

Traffic Safety

"Accidents destroy good will," the handbook explained. So drivers were expected to obey all traffic rules and regulations—and with courtesy. ("Always give the other fellow the right of way.") A Good Humor man would never allow children to run across the street to reach his truck: He always brought the ice cream to them. Children were also forbidden from climbing or riding on the truck, for fear of injury.

Sales Equipment

Each Good Humor man was issued a truck to drive. (Or, in some cases, a sales car, trailer, tricycle vending cart, etc.) At the end of every day, the truck had to be thoroughly washed until it sparkled, and kept immaculate inside as well. "Which restaurant would you prefer to patronize?" asked the Handbook. "One that is neat, clean, and decorated in good taste, or one that appears greasy, sloppy, and unsanitary? *Your* customers will feel the same way."

The Uniform

The Good Humor Corporation provided salesmen each day with a clean-and-pressed, easily recognizable uniform: blue bow tie, white pants and jacket, shoulder belt, money changer, name plate, and a Marine-style hat. The drivers were inspected before making their rounds to make sure their shoes were polished to a shine. On hot days, the drivers could remove their jackets, but short-sleeved, open-neck shirts were not allowed.

Sales Procedure

"Smile and salute, at the same time saying, 'Good Afternoon,' or 'Good Evening,' and 'May I Serve You?' advised the handbook. Since most customers were children, drivers were encouraged to "treat them with sincerity, respect and KINDNESS; learn their names, where they live, their grades in school, their hobbies. . . try to remember what flavors each individual child likes . . ." Most important: "Protect them at all times." In other words, be a true friend. Many of the drivers Good Humor hired were either fathers or grandfathers, since these men often knew best how to talk and be patient with children.

"Surliness [is] not toler-
ated."

Fame and Fortune

Kind. Courteous. Friendly.
Enthusiastic. Dedicated.

The Good Humor men
earned these glowing
descriptions—and more.
Time magazine called them
urban folk heroes, for the
drivers truly cared about,
and took care of, their customers and the neighbor-
hoods in which they lived.
Good Humor vendors were
known to rescue kittens
from trees and assist car-
accident victims. Once, after a flood in Connecticut, they
gave free ice cream to the survivors. They even helped
Long Island police shut down a counterfeit money ring!
Dogs became the Good Humor man's best friend: They
panted and wagged and chased the trucks down the street
whenever they heard the bells, in hopes that their owners
would buy them ice cream, too.

Good Humor ice cream and its gallant vendors
became world-renowned. Newspaper and magazine articles were written about them. Cartoons and comic strips
featured them. So did radio programs, Broadway shows,
comedians' jokes, and hundreds of movies. One film
called *The Good Humor Man* was produced by Columbia
Pictures in 1950. The inspiration? A Good Humor truck

**Good Humor Jokes
of the 1940s**
Did you hear the one
about the cannibal
chief with the sweet
tooth? For dessert he
always ate a Good
Humor man! Say, how
about the man who
crashed his car through
a schoolyard fence? He
thought he was follow-
ing the road's white
line. Actually, it was a
Good Humor truck leak-
ing vanilla ice cream!

parked outside the Hollywood studio every day at the same time, dishing out ice cream to movie execs and extras alike.

But all good things come to an end—even the Good Humor men. By the 1960s, only fifteen hundred Good Humor trucks still rumbled on the road. By the 1970s, that number had been cut in half. The trucks were phased out completely in 1976. High gasoline and insurance prices were one reason. Noise pollution was another. By then, many cities had enacted antinoise ordinances, which made the chimes on the Good Humor trucks illegal. (A group of kids in Jackson, Mississippi, were so outraged about one ordinance, they sued the city for a "trillion" dollars to keep their neighborhood Good Humor man in business. Rather than fight the expensive lawsuit, the Jackson city council made an exception for the vendor so his bells could peal again.)

Customers had changed their habits, too. Now they were

In the 1950s and '60s, kids had a chance to taste-test new Good Humor flavors—over three thousand flavors in all. The top-secret recipes were locked in a heavily guarded safe. Every week, April through September, the radio commercial advertising that week's flavor was sent in code to stations across the country. On the day the commercial was scheduled to air, a Good Humor official would call each station at the last minute, sending announcers the decoding information. Kids gave a thumbs-up to many scrumptious flavors. Thumbs-down flavors? Licorice, prune, kumquat, and—heehaw!—chili con carne.

The sign reads: <u>Join the summer book club now</u>. A school reading program? Library Literacy event? Nope. It's the Ice Cream Truck Summer Book Club! This cool club is the brainchild of Matt Lamstein, an ice cream vendor who wanted to bring the magic of ice cream and reading to the kids of Portsmouth, New Hampshire. Any kid along Lamstein's 40-mile route can join: when you see his truck trundling by, just stop him and ask for a membership card. For each book read, a free ice cream prize is earned. "Read one book, you get a small ice cream treat," explains Lamstein. "Read three books, you get an even bigger treat. Read six books or more, and you can have any frozen dessert you want—on the house!" Lamstein also puts the readers' names on the Ice Cream Truck Book Club Honor Roll, taped onto the ice cream freezer. What a sweet way to spend the summer . . . reading good books and eating ice cream!

more interested in buying ice cream in supermarket or convenience stores, rather than from the door-to-door delivery trucks. So the last of the Good Humor men hung up their hats for the last time and jingled off into the sunset . . .

But the delicious ice cream products live on. Today, Burt's basement invention is part of Good Humor-Breyer's of Greenbay, Wisconsin, the largest ice cream company on the planet. The company boasts hundreds of delicious frozen novelty and packaged ice cream products—such as the Klondike Bar, Popsicle, and Fat Free Fudgsicle brands—and more than two thousand good-humored men and women, employees who work hard even without the bells to bring you a little "happiness on a handle."

Section 5

FROM COW TO CONE:
Ice Cream
Production

A dairy science student connects an automatic milking machine to the udder of each cow in a university "milking parlor." The raw milk is pumped directly into a storage tank and then into refrigerated, stainless steel tanker trucks, where it is rushed to the nearest ice cream factory within 24 hours.

Photo credit: Courtesy Les Ferriera, California Polytechnic State University, San Luis Obispo

Assembly line workers prepare freshly-baked cones for packing machines that will automatically box them in protective packaging, ready for transport to grocery stores, supermarkets, and ice cream shops across the country.

Photo credit: Courtesy Joy Cone Company

• 12 •

The Deep Freeze: How Ice Cream is Made

... They passed a door in the wall. "No time to go in!" shouted Mr. Wonka. "Press on! Press on!" They passed another door [of the factory], then another and another ... HOT ICE CREAMS FOR COLD DAYS, it said on the next door. "<u>Extremely</u> useful in the winter," said Mr. Wonka, rushing on. "Hot ice cream warms you up no end in freezing weather."

—*Charlie and the Chocolate Factory,*
by Roald Dahl, 1964.

Willy Wonka, that fictional magician of chocolate, had no trouble conjuring up fantastical ice creams. And hundreds of years ago, when frozen desserts were a rarity, ice cream's creation must have tasted like magic. Today, we know that the making of ice cream requires a lot more than hocus-pocus. The process is a scientific and technological one that begins not with the wave of a magic wand, but with a sweet and docile "moo" ...

The Udder Truth

"Producing good ice cream is like building a house," explains Professor Les Ferreira, head of the Dairy Science Department at California Polytechnic State University in San Luis Obispo, California. "A well-built home needs good materials and good construction. You also need a solid foundation. For delicious ice cream, that foundation is the cow."

Ferreira should know. In addition to his degrees in dairy science, he was raised on a dairy farm and learned how to milk before he was old enough to attend school. As a child and teen, he was active in 4-H programs and the Future Farmers of America (FFA).

"A healthy cow means high milk quality, which equals high-quality ice cream," Ferreira continues. He makes his way through the free-stall barns that house the herd at the university. He stops to scratch one cow gently behind the ears, then slaps another affectionately on the rump. "A high-producing milk cow is like an athlete. She must stay in excellent physical health to give the best milk. So each cow has her own diet, exercise, and training plan."

When it's time for the cows to be milked, they are ushered into their individual stations in the milking parlor. No, not the formal parlor of your great-great-grandmother's day. The parlors in most dairies and farms today are a study in stainless steel, with polished stalls, state-of-the-art machinery, and tiled floors—all squeaky-clean and gleaming. The completely automated equipment produces a soothing background hum, and the parlor at Cal Poly has a mild, pleasant smell of fresh grass, warm milk—and cow.

Once the cows are in place, the teats of the udders are washed with an idoine solution and dried with disposable towels. Then tubes from a "pulsating milk machine" are attached. This machine includes a mechanism that helps to stimulate the udder to release as much milk as possible.

"Each cow has her own name and number, and wears what we call a 'transponder' around her neck," says Ferreira. "The transponders send out radio signals to our main computer, linking information about each cow's milking session to her records. The computer measures things like how long it takes to milk her and how many pounds of milk she's giving. If there are deviations in what's usual for her, we investigate immediately. Cows are a dairyman's livelihood: if they are sick, it can affect the product and our reputation."

In the old days, farmers used to milk each cow by hand, a process that took twenty minutes or more per cow. Now most farms and dairies use machines, similar to those at Cal Poly, that can milk a cow in about three minutes.

The warm, raw milk flows through the cow's teats into the tubes of the milking machine, and directly into a pipe.

It is then pumped into refrigerated storage tanks, where it is chilled within an hour to about 35 degrees F. The milk is never touched by human hands, and has little contact with air. This keeps bacteria from getting into the liquid

---

The average California cow gives 2,305 gallons of milk each year during her milking cycle. This means 128 kids could have a glass of milk each day for ten months—from only one cow! To produce this much liquid, cows must daily eat about 41 pounds of feed and drink between 25-60 gallons of water: an entire bathtub's worth!

---

and spoiling it. Dairy managers and USDA inspectors test the milk for impurities and bacteria, and keep their eye on the facility to make sure the process runs smoothly. They expect everything to be clean and dry, safe and sanitary. "Attention to detail," concludes Ferreira, "is what helps create a wholesome, good-tasting product."

An Amusement Park for Ice Cream

Cal Poly State University uses the milk produced in its dairy to make cheese, yogurt, and ice cream for its students. But at most farms and dairies, raw milk slated for ice cream is pumped directly from the storage tanks into stainless-steel tankers—refrigerated tank trucks that can hold four thousand gallons of milk—and hustled within twenty-four hours to the nearest ice cream factory.

Each factory has its own delicious recipes for creating different mixes and flavors of the dessert. But the multistep production process is similar, no matter how large or small the company.

The factory is like an amusement park for ice cream: Over the course of several hours, the cow's milk and other essential ingredients will whiz through pipes, tilt-a-whirl in vats, and roller-coaster their way along conveyor belts, transforming into a delectable frozen dessert. So get your tickets! The fun begins in . . .

The Blend Tank

Have you ever helped to bake a cake using a handheld mixer? It's the best way to blend the ingredients thoroughly. The principle behind the blend tank is the same. Ingredients such as milk, cream, eggs, liquid sugar, and flavorings are pumped into the tank, creating the ice cream mix or base; then a high-speed beater churns the mix round and round. A special chef called the mix master oversees the entire recipe and process, to ensure the mixing and measuring is followed precisely.

"There are two main kinds of mixes," says Jim McCoy, president of McConnell's Fine Ice Creams, Inc., in Santa Barbara, California, which *Time* magazine once called "the best ice cream in the world." "White, or vanilla, is the base used for most flavors that manufacturers produce. That's because so many fruits, flavorings, and colorings can be added to it, making hundreds of different kinds of ice creams such as Bordeaux Strawberry, Peppermint Stick, or our gold-medal-winning French Vanilla.

"The second base mix is chocolate. The recipe for this mix is identical to the white—except you add the obvious: chocolate. [This can be done with cocoa powder, liquors, syrups, etc.] This is the base we use for many chocolaty flavors, such as our rich Chocolate Raspberry Truffle and Swiss Chocolate Chip. We make our white mix in the mornings, and our chocolate base in the afternoons. The blend tank is thoroughly cleaned and sanitized in between."

The Pasteurizer

After blending, the mix is pumped through another pipe into a machine called the pasteurizer. (McConnell's and many other ice cream plants pasteurize the milk before it goes into the blend tank. Either way is fine.)

In the 1860s, the French chemist Louis Pasteur learned that disease-causing bacteria found in foods could be destroyed by exposing those foods to high temperatures for short periods of time. This treatment—called pasteurization—works especially well on dairy products, preventing bacteria from damaging the flavor and texture of the ice cream and keeping customers from becoming ill.

Once in the Pasteurizer, the mix is heated to about 175 degrees F (80 degrees C) for twenty-five seconds. Zap! go the bacteria—but amazingly, the mix is not harmed in any way. Then, the hot mix is shot through a pipe for another wild ride in . . .

The Homogenizer

When your great-great-grandmother was a child, milk was delivered door-to-door by horse-drawn wagons. The horses wore rubber shoes to keep the clippety-clop of their hooves quiet in the predawn hours. When the lady of the house gathered in the bottles of milk left on her doorstep, she would notice a thick, rich layer of cream floating on top. One of her first jobs of the morning was to stir the liquid, gradually reblending the cream.

In a way, your great-great-granny was the first "homogenizer."

Cream is much lighter than milk because it's made of large fat globules. These globules are what cause the cream to rise to the top of the fluid and hang there, "kind of like those fat inner-tube things you might float around on in a swimming pool," jokes a spokesperson from Ben & Jerry's Ice Cream.

The homogenizer pushes and squishes the globules with high-pressure pistons and cylinders. This breaks the fat up into fine particles, blending them with the other ingredients. Homogenization keeps the rich fat from rising to the top and becoming butter during the churning of the freezing process. It also assures that the ice cream will be smooth, creamy, and uniform in taste and texture.

After homogenization is completed, the hot mix is immediately zipped into refrigerated storage tanks, where its temperature is reduced to 34–40 degrees F—just above freezing. The mix, which now has the consistency of a milk shake, remains in these tanks for four to twelve hours. This is called "curing" or "aging." Cheese and wine are always aged before consumption, and the reason is the same: The aging process intensifies flavor. Curing also improves the body and texture of the mix, making it ready for the next roller-coaster ride.

The Freezing Process

Gone are the days when Jacob Fussell and dozens of workers hand-cranked batches of ice cream until their arms were weak and trembly from exhaustion. Today, the freezing process is computerized and completely automated.

"There are two types of ice cream freezers," explains McCoy, "continuous and batch. Continuous freezers are used when making large quantities of a particular flavor. They feed a steady flow of mix and air into the freezer chamber. After freezing, a consistent flow of the ice cream is pushed out the other end, ready for packaging.

"The batch freezer is used mostly in small plants producing small amounts of ice cream in a short period of time."

Ed Kruse, whose father started Blue Bell Ice Cream in Brenham, Texas, remembers the family making a ten-gallon container of ice cream about every twenty minutes in the 1930s using a batch-type freezer.

"We got our first continuous freezer in 1936," Kruse says. "... [the ice cream] continuously flowed out of a stainless-steel pipe. I can recall my dad saying—and I wasn't but six years of age—'Who will eat all this ice cream?' We made eighty gallons an hour with that machine." Today, the creamery produces thousands of gallons per hour, and Krause has never given another thought as to

The first commercial batch freezer was invented in 1905 by Emery Thompson, the manager of a soda fountain in a New York City department store. It was also known as a "brine freezer" because of the salt solution used in the refrigeration process. The continuous freezer, first patented in 1913, became commercially successful in 1926 when Clarence Vogt perfected the earlier designs. It has been widely used in ice cream plants since the 1930s.

The first course in the country on making ice cream was taught at Penn State in 1892. The school has offered these delicious short courses regularly since 1925. Today, the college boasts the largest university creamery in the nation, with 3.5 million pounds of milk being processed annually. They make about 120,000 gallons a year of their famous ice cream in a wide variety of flavors—many named after school coaches and professors.

who will eat it all!

The basic process and results of both the batch and continuous freezers are the same. As the mix freezes, revolving blades called dashers (remember Nancy Johnson?) constantly whip the product. Milk, cream, and liquid sugar all contain water. When water freezes, it turns into ice crystals. Whipping the mixture breaks down these crystals into small pieces. This keeps the final product smooth.

The dashers are also essential for whipping air into the product. Air creates a soft, light, and smooth dessert. Too little air in the mix produces a heavy, soggy ice cream which is difficult to flavor. Too much air can create a dry, dull product, much like fresh powdery snow. Without any air at all, the ice cream freezes into a solid, inedible mass. Air also increases the volume of the mix: one gallon of mix transforms into two gallons of ice cream—all because of air.

When the liquid ice cream reaches a temperature of 22–26 degrees F, fruits, nuts, chocolate chips, candies, marshmallows, etc., are dropped or injected into it to make specific flavors. The ice cream is still semisoft, and it's easy for machines to blend the chunks evenly throughout.

The dessert then wends its way through the freezer pipes into the carton filler, where a precisely measured amount of ice cream is squirted into containers traveling along a conveyor belt. A lid is automatically plopped on and the containers are shrink-wrapped in plastic, a half dozen at a time. The packaged ice cream is then ready for its last ride to the . . .

Hardening Room

This room is actually a huge freezer with a slick, ice-covered floor and wall-to-wall ice cream containers. The cartons are stacked onto pallets and stored here for 6–8 hours to allow time for the ice cream to harden completely.

At Dreyer's, the production-floor workers who labor in this area are among the highest paid: that's because the temperature controls of the hardening room are set at a numbing *30 degrees below zero.* (If there's a breeze, the windchill factor drops to −50 degrees F.) Everyone who enters the hardening room for longer than a few seconds must do so dressed for an arctic winter. Thickly padded gloves, coveralls, pants, jackets, and hoods—which resemble the bulky space suits worn by American astronauts—are a necessity if one doesn't want to freeze to death within a few minutes.

"We used to have a worker back in the 1960s and '70s who was a real practical joker," says McConnell's

"In the old days," remembers McConnell's Fine Ice Cream president Jim McCoy, "it was required by law that we have an axe and a buzzer inside the hardening room and storage freezer. That way, if a worker got trapped inside, he could either punch the buzzer—alerting the people outside—or use the axe to hack his way out. Nowadays, there's no way someone can be locked in. It's required by law that all freezer doors be designed to open from the inside. My wife still gets nervous, though. When she visits our plant on the weekends to snitch some ice cream for a party, she unlocks the door, and takes the lock inside with her so no one can lock her in!"

Jim McCoy. "On the days we gave tours of the McConnell's plant to school kids, this employee would zip into the walk-in freezer—where the temp was 20 below!—right before the kids were ushered through. And there he'd be when they walked inside, sitting on a chair, reading a newspaper—with his shirt off! Oh, how the kids would squeal and exclaim!"

After the ice cream has hardened, the containers are moved and stacked in another freezer called the cold box, where the temperature is a balmy −10 degrees F. (The core of each ice cream container is now about −6 degrees.) The cold box houses the ice cream until the next day, when it is shipped to grocery and convenience stores via delivery trucks. Dreyer's Union City plant alone houses one million gallons of ice cream in its cold box or warehouse, turning that amount over twice a month.

The roller-coaster ride is now over—at least for you: some ice cream plants run twenty-four hours a day! Of course, no visit to any amusement park is complete without a cone or dish filled with luscious ice cream. Don't forget to ask for your free sample on the way home!

Ice-cream-production plants, large and small, must follow strict public health laws. Quality-control experts and inspectors see that the equipment and work environment is safe and spick-and-span, and that the ice cream is consistently of the highest quality. To ensure this, workers on the production floor must wear lab coats, hair nets, beard nets (!), and special safety shoes with protective coverings. In some cases, hard hats must be worn. No jewelry is allowed, and shoes usually worn inside the plant are not allowed out of the facility. This is a far cry from some of the ice cream plants of the late 1800s, where, as one manufacturer recalled, "the ice cream makers were often drunk or chewed tobacco—some of which got into the mix!"

• 13 •

The Man with the Million-Dollar Taste Buds

"I am hungry," said Zelmo. "I need ice cream."
"I never knew they ate ice cream on Mars," said Stanley.
"That is all we eat," said Zelmo. "I make ice cream on Mars, but we have only three flavors: fleenzil, uplaloo, and plinkee."
"Like chocolate, vanilla, and strawberry?" asked Stanley.
"Almost the same," said Zelmo.

—from *The Banana Split from Outer Space*
by Catherine Siracusa, Hyperion, 1995.

"What do you want to be when you grow up?"

That's a favorite question of parents and teachers . . . and probably your Great-Aunt Gertrude, who asks it at every family reunion while annoyingly pinching your cheek.

So what *do* you want to be? Doctor, lawyer? Rock star, librarian? Firefighter, astronaut?

The next time Great-Auntie looms in, pincher-fingers ready, why not announce that you'd like to be . . . an ice cream taster?

Yes, there really *is* a job where you eat ice cream every day . . . and get *paid* for it! John Harrison of Dreyer's Grand Ice Cream can vouch for that: He's their official taste tester. During his career, he's sampled hundreds of flavors and well over 150 million gallons of the frozen dessert. In fact, he's so good at his job, Harrison's taste buds are insured for one million dollars.

So what's a typical day like for the man with the coolest job in the world? Grab a spoon, and let's find out . . .

Temper, Temper

"We're all kids when it comes to ice cream," Harrison says, as he straightens his signature bow tie and dons an immaculate white lab coat. He tucks a special gold-plated teaspoon and a thermometer into his pocket, important tasting tools he'll need later. "That's why I enjoy my job so much. The ice cream, of course, tastes good. But it also conjures up good memories of good times: family, friends, celebrations." He grabs his briefcase and is ready to go.

Wait a minute. No breakfast? Not even a gulp of hot coffee before dashing out the door?

Harrison shakes his head. "Coffee has caffeine, and caffeine clogs the taste buds. I also don't want to risk burning my tongue. I usually start the day with only a cup of warm, decaffeinated herbal tea. I need my taste buds to be fresh. I don't drink alcohol or smoke, and I avoid eating spicy foods during the week, especially those with onions, garlic, curry, or cayenne. These flavors can linger in the taste buds for twelve hours or more."

Does this mean he can't ever eat pizza?

"Only on the weekends," Harrison answers with a

smile. "That's when I let my hair down. Pepperoni pizza. Thai food. You name it. I love to cook—and to eat!"

By 7:30 A.M., when taste buds are at their peak, Harrison has arrived at the Dreyer's plant in Union City, California. The twenty different flavors he will taste this morning were all made yesterday. Plant managers plucked sample containers—sixty in all—from the beginning, middle, and end of the production runs, setting them aside for him in the lab freezer. The ice cream made in these runs will not be shipped until Harrison gives them the green light. His taste buds, explains Tyler Johnson, Vice President of Marketing, "are the final quality-control check for [Dreyer's] products before they reach the consumer."

Harrison takes out the first carton—vanilla—and sets it on the counter.

"I always begin with the lighter flavors," he says, "working up to the heavier, intense, more complex ones, such as mint chip. But first it's important to temper, or warm up, the ice cream. If it's too cold, it will deaden the effectiveness of my taste buds. It will actually freeze or numb them. You get more flavor from warmer ice cream, which is why some kids like to stir it, creating ice cream 'soup.'"

When ice cream is pulled from the freezer at home, its temperature is about 5 degrees F. Harrison tastes his samples at 10–12 degrees F to maximize the flavors—both good and bad.

While the ice cream is tempering, Harrison talks a little about his background.

"My great-grandfather owned two ice cream parlors in New York City in the early 1900s," he says. "My grandfather started the first dairy co-op in Tennessee, and my uncle owned an ice cream factory in the South. Even my dad was in the business: He owned a dairy-ingredients factory in Atlanta." He chuckles. "My blood runs 16 percent butterfat!"

Harrison himself has worked in the industry for more than thirty years. In 1997, the American Tasting Institute bestowed upon him the award of Master Taster of the Year. Now he's ready again this morning to put that experience and his famous taste buds to work.

Ice cream comes in more flavors than any other food. An ice cream shop in Venezuela, Helados Coromoto, is listed in the Guinness Book of World Records as serving the most flavors: a scooping 550! The flavor list takes up an entire back wall of the parlor; and 100 of those are available every day. The speciality of the house is pabellon criollo, which is similar to the national dish of shredded beef, black beans, rice, and plantains (a type of banana).

The Three S's

Harrison takes out a special ice cream knife and cuts the package of vanilla into thirds, laying open the three sections on the counter.

"Tasting begins with the eyes," he says. "The first thing I look for in a good ice cream is its appearance or color. I need to ask myself: Is the color attractive? Delicate? Does the product have the color expected from that flavor?

Color affects how we *think* food should taste. No matter how good a dish of pasta smells, you might not eat it if the spaghetti is blue."

If there are added ingredients—such as fruit or chocolate chips—now is the time for Harrison to make sure the pieces are evenly distributed throughout the ice cream.

After analyzing the ice cream's appearance, Harrison is ready for a taste test. He removes the gold-plated teaspoon from his pocket and skims it across the top of the open container, where the ice cream is the warmest. Then he turns the spoon upside down, plopping the small scoop of dessert directly onto his tongue instead of the roof of his mouth. Then it's time for what Harrison calls the Three S's: Swirl, Smack, and Spit.

"I swirl the ice cream very quickly around my mouth," Harrison says, "completely coating my taste buds. Then I smack my mouth several times, very fast. This warms and aerates the ice cream even more, releasing maximum flavor."

Harrison is now also tasting with his nose as he breathes out, judging the "top note" or aroma of the ice cream. It's the olfactory nerves that so strongly heighten our sense of taste. That's why when you have a head cold, most foods—except super sweet or spicy ones—taste bland. The sinus nerve has swelled, blocking the top note.

People who lose their sense of smell because of injury or illness almost never enjoy eating, because an important taste sensor has been damaged.

"If a lady wearing perfume walks by while I'm tasting," Harrison says, "I need to take a break. The strong scent can overwhelm or deaden my olfactory nerves for a few minutes, and I can't smell the top note."

While swirling and smacking the spoonful, Harrison is looking for balance in the cream, natural flavors, and sweetening ingredients.

"The experience needs to be well-rounded," he explains. "There should be no 'spikes' in the ice cream: no single ingredient that stands out stronger than the rest. If one does, then something is wrong. If an ice cream tastes too sweet, then I know the butterfat content is too low. If I get a thick film on my tongue, then I know the butterfat content is too high. Both situations throw the ice cream out of balance, and make it an unacceptable product by our standards.

"Well-rounded texture and body are essential, too. Good ice cream has to be smooth and creamy—not coarse, icy, or gummy. Premium quality ice cream is expensive. The consumer has a right to demand top quality for top price."

Tongue Twister

When the swirling and smacking is complete— the whole process takes about 3–5 seconds— Harrison neatly spits the

The 5 Most Popular Ice Cream Flavors in America:
1. Vanilla
2. Chocolate
3. Butter pecan
4. Strawberry
5. Neapolitan

sample of ice cream into the bucket.

Hold on, you might exclaim. He doesn't actually get to *swallow* the ice cream?

"Rarely," admits Harrison, "because it's not necessary to the tasting process." Here's why:

Our tongues are covered with *nine thousand* taste buds. Each bud has ten to fifteen receptacles that send messages whizzing up to our brains, telling us we're eating something sweet (like ice cream), or salty (chicken soup); sour (lime Jell-O), or bitter (unsweetened chocolate). Taste buds on the tip of our tongue taste the sweet stuff; buds on the sides recognize salt or sour; bitter is tasted in the back. So unless an ice cream is bitter (which it shouldn't be!), Harrison doesn't need to swallow it. He only takes a gulp when testing new flavors, because he must evaluate the aftereffect of the product.

"Besides," he concludes, "if I swallowed all sixty samples each morning, I'd get full. And once you get full, you lose the sharpness for tasting. I'd probably get fat, too. Sure, I'm stocky, but I've always been—it's not because of the ice cream—and who'd trust a skinny ice cream taster?"

Over the next four to five hours, Harrison will move along the counter, sampling flavor after flavor. Swirl, smack, spit . . . Swirl, smack, spit. If he tastes a flavor that is "off"—defective or out of balance—he'll stop to rinse out his mouth with water, eat an unsalted cracker, rinse once more, then start again. He is accompanied by a backup taster, a kind of taster-in-training.

"It's called team tasting," he says. "We have an ongoing conversation about the ice creams, grading them on scoring sheets which are then given to the ice cream makers in the lab. The results are compiled, and the employees in each workshift (there are three shifts each day) are graded for consistency and quality in the desserts they've produced. Workers receive bonuses if their scores are high."

After a full morning of sampling, Harrison is suffering from what is known in the business as "flavor fatigue." "My taste buds have reached a saturation point," he says, "and can't judge flavors efficiently anymore. So now I finally eat breakfast—or lunch—one with mild flavors, of course."

Does this mean Harrison is calling it a day?

"Oh, no," he replies. "There's a lot more to do before quitting time."

True Confessions

Aside from his tasting role at Dreyer's, Harrison wears another hat: overseeing production of more than 25 million gallons of ice cream at plants across the country. He's on the road constantly, helping to train tasters ("preparing to give them the keys to the kingdom!"), testing the shelf life of products, investigating secondary suppliers for ingredients, and giving endless tasting demonstrations to the public. He also works in the marketing department, doing research and development for new ice cream products.

"When I go out to eat, I never pass up a dessert tray," Harrison says with a laugh, "because I'm always on the lookout for new taste ideas and new combinations. One time, I was sitting with a bowl of vanilla ice cream and there was a cookie on the plate. I thought to myself: *Why not put the cookie in the ice cream?* That's how the first Cookies 'N Cream was invented!"

Harrison has helped to develop 75–100 new ice cream

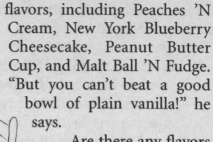

flavors, including Peaches 'N Cream, New York Blueberry Cheesecake, Peanut Butter Cup, and Malt Ball 'N Fudge. "But you can't beat a good bowl of plain vanilla!" he says.

Are there any flavors of ice cream Harrison *doesn't* like?

"I don't much care for Green Tea," he confesses. "It's a popular flavor among Asians—we sell it in a three-gallon tub size!—as they tend to prefer ice cream that's less sweet. I also didn't care much for mint chocolate chip the first time I tasted it. Then I tried it after a meal, and it was deeelicious—like an after-dinner mint.

"Some ice creams are a surprise. Once I tried an ice cream with jalapeno peppers. My brain literally twitched when I tasted it, because it was cold and hot at the same time."

Is there a right way to eat ice cream?

"Only if you're an official taste tester," Harrison says. "Otherwise, you can chew, bite, drink, or lick it. Licking, in my opinion, is the best. It prolongs the experience, and it's easier on sensitive teeth."

Like most Americans, after a hard week at the office, Harrison likes to go home and relax with his wife, and visit with his five adult children—all of whom were "unofficial tasters" while growing up. ("My son Van is a dairy science major in college. He's going to be my ice cream man!") One of his favorite weekend pastimes is . . . making ice cream!

"I like to make banana and walnut," he says, "adding ribbons of goodies just before it's completely frozen. I eat about a quart a week—off duty, of course."

Last but not least, what advice does he have for kids who want to grow up to be taste testers just like him?

"It's cool to stay in school," he recommends, quoting an old slogan. It's an oldie but a goodie: Making and tasting ice cream requires a background in chemistry, zoology, bacteriology, etc, so a college diploma is essential.

"You might also practice doing blind taste tests with your friends," Harrison adds. "Have each person bring a different brand of vanilla or chocolate ice cream to your house in a brown paper bag. As you taste, analyze elements such as appearance, texture, color, aroma. This will help to develop your palate—and it's delicious fun, too!"

Sound advice from the man with the sweetest job in the world.

TEN WEIRDEST ICE CREAM FLAVORS

1. Mashed potato and bacon
2. Tuna Fish
3. Fried Pork Rind
4. Chili con Carne
5. Garlic
6. Sauerkraut
7. Horseradish and Beer
8. Mustard
9. Dill Pickle
10. Ketchup

The Blizzard Wizards: Creating Ice Cream Flavors

When August sizzles and sidewalks bake,
I'm a blizzard wizard with magic to make.
To stop the hot, here's my trick:
It's winter frozen on a stick!
My instant, super-cooling system
In so many flavors, I can't list 'em.
Every bite's a cold wind blowing,
Skating, sledding, look! It's snowing!
But hurry up and eat some more.
You have to finish it before
It changes into drip and slush . . .
Too late—
My magic's melted mush!

—"Blizzard Wizard" by Ellen Kelley

Ben Cohen was a college dropout turned pottery teacher who had driven an ice cream truck in high school. Jerry Greenfield got his degree in premed, putting himself through college by scooping ice cream in the university cafeteria. Buddies since meeting in a seventh-grade gym class, they thought it would be fun to start a business together. Their first choice, a bagel delivery service, turned to burnt toast when they couldn't afford the equipment. Their second choice proved better: twenty years after these blizzard wizards started their ice cream company with a $5 investment, Ben & Jerry's Homemade, Inc.—well-known for its unique flavors riddled with scrumptious chunks of add-ins—was worth $200 million.

Fill 'Er Up!

Sporting T-shirts, jeans, and unruly hair, Ben and Jerry were not your white-uniformed, starched-hat soda jerks of yesteryear. But they did share the same passion for ice cream as their scooping ancestors. As a kid, Ben loved "inventing" flavors by smashing chunks of cookies and candy bits into his bowls of ice cream!

In 1977, when the young men were in their mid-twenties, Ben and Jerry spent five dollars to take an ice-cream-making correspondence course (similar to going to school by mail!) through Penn State University. They passed with flying flavors. After nixing Saratoga Springs, New York, as their first-choice site for an ice cream parlor (they discovered the town already had one), they headed north to Burlington, Vermont. Bankers approached for a loan had their doubts: The Vermont winters—and summers—were so chilly, they wondered if anyone would warm up to the idea of ice cream. In fact, the state was the only one out of fifty not to feature a single Baskin-Robbins! Still, the town boasted a large student population from the nearby University of Vermont. The bankers relented, and a small loan was granted.

Ben and Jerry started their new business on a shoe-string: they bought a used, hand-crank White Mountain freezer, and used restaurant equipment. They set up shop in one-half of an old gas station, working day and night—even sleeping in the drafty building—to get the store and their recipes ready for the Grand Opening.

May 5, 1978: The Big Day arrived. Ben and Jerry flung open their doors to the waiting crowd. Their rich, super-premium ice creams were a super success. People flocked to the store all summer long, enjoying licks and drips while watching free movies screened on the outside of a nearby building, or listening to a pianist who tickled his ivories in exchange for scoops.

Over the years, Ben and Jerry expanded their company, packaging their ice cream in pints, and distributing it to restaurants and supermarkets. They were able to move out of the old rented gas station, building their own company headquarters and a gigantic manufacturing plant—which U.S. News and World Report called "one of the top ten tours in the country"—and offering their dessert delights in eleven countries. They also committed the company to a number of political and social activities. Among them, five of their 170 "scoop shops"—ice cream stores—are run by nonprofit groups that employ troubled teens and the disadvantaged to help get them on their feet again.

But Ben & Jerry's Homemade, Inc. is best known for its chunky flavors with the funky names, such as Cherry Garcia, Chubby Hubby, and the extrafudgy Phish Food.

Who comes up with these delicious flavors? And with the deliciously humorous names to match? Are the blizzard wizards still waving their magic wands over every single pint of what *Time* magazine once called "The Best Ice Cream in the World?"

Meet Mary Kamm. She knows the answers to these questions . . . and more.

The Sweetest Game in Town

"I'm the director of Research and Development here at Ben & Jerry's, but everyone calls me Coach," Kamm says with a chuckle. "That's because I oversee a team of flavor developers. Our game is to invent new ice creams."

In the early days, Ben and Jerry created all the flavors themselves. Ben, who has sinus problems, was unable to taste the typically mild ice cream flavors, such as chocolate or vanilla. To intensify these desserts, he continued his boyhood ploy of plopping in extra goodies: fudge and cherries, toffee and nuts, cookies and peanut butter. But as Ben and Jerry's company grew—from eight flavors to more than fifty—so did their responsibilities. An official department was needed to develop what Kamm calls the Three P's: new Products, new Processes to make those products, and new Packaging to better advertise and sell them.

Of course, the Three P's would be nowhere without . . . People.

"My department," explains Kamm, "is made up of a diverse group of engineers, chefs, scientists, sensory analysts, and accountants [people who figure out costs]. I have a degree in food science, which is a type of chemistry degree focused on food." Kamm was the first female manager at the Nestlé Candy Company and worked in the food industry for fourteen years before coming to Ben & Jerry's. Now she's in charge of creating five to ten new ice cream flavors every year.

Only *five*, you say? Easy as . . . pie à la mode, right?

Wrong. Kamm and her team take this business seriously, and will spend twelve months developing new flavors you'll gobble up in five minutes.

On Your Mark . . .

"Each year, in January," Kamm begins, "the marketing department at Ben & Jerry's gives us a list of our products that are selling well—and those that are not. Then we come up with between one hundred fifty and two hundred new flavor concepts. We get these ideas three ways.

"First, we all take a yearly dessert tour. This is one of the best parts of our job, because we travel around to lots of restaurants tasting all the trendy desserts. We sample between 200 and 300 new desserts a week!

"Next, we sample new trends in the candy, cookie, and beverage markets—the beverage industry has always been a pioneer of unique flavors—to see what might translate well to ice cream.

"Last, we occasionally use ideas we get from our customers. Cherry Garcia and Chunky Monkey, two of our more famous flavors, were inspired by consumers."

Chubby Hubby, introduced in 1995, is another good example.

"Two women who worked in an office together wanted to play a trick on one of their coworkers," Kamm explained in an on-line interview. "They sent us a letter, telling us about it. The worker had bragged that he knew all of the Ben & Jerry's flavors, so the women made up the name Chubby Hubby and asked if he had ever tasted it. He went wild because he couldn't find it anywhere!" Kamm's team thought it was a funny story and a cool name, and developed a flavor to go with it. The result was a vanilla malt ice cream with ripples of fudge and peanut butter, studded with chocolate-covered pretzels filled with *more* peanut butter. The pranksters not only had their fictitious ice cream turned to reality, they will receive free Ben & Jerry's ice cream as long as Chubby Hubby stays on the market.

> Ben & Jerry's Chunky Monkey ice cream (banana ice cream with walnuts and chocolate hunks) needed a name change when it hit the market in Japan because people took its moniker literally!

Do kids ever send in ideas?

"Oh, yes," Kamm says, "although none of those has ever made it past the brainstorming stage. But once, several of us visited a middle school in Vermont to talk with a class about the science, chemistry, and engineering skills needed to make ice cream. We held an ice cream contest, and made one pint of each of the students' ice cream ideas—twenty in

all. The kids went nuts! One of the weirdest flavors had a Cheez Whiz swirl. The winning ice cream was a chocolate-covered trail mix combo."

Get Set . . .

After Kamm's department has conjured up 150+ flavor concepts they feel might work, the marketing department writes descriptions of the potential products and has customers read them.

"An outside firm hires the consumers for us," Kamm says. "These people fill out lengthy questionaires before they're chosen for our concept and taste tests. They can be men or women—although we try to keep it 50-50—between the ages of 18 and 60. But they *must* be superpremium ice cream lovers. This means they must like ice cream with a high butterfat content. They must also earn between fifteen thousand and a hundred thousand dollars a year. Superpremium ice creams cost more than premium or regular brands, so our test consumers must be the type of people who would actually buy, and could afford to buy, our ice cream."

The consumers chosen for the test read the flavor descriptions on their lists. Then they pick the three ice creams they'd be most likely to eat. Kamm's department narrows these choices down to fifty new flavors.

"By March 1," Kamm continues, "we're ready to begin commercial development. That means we go into the lab and make prototypes of the ice cream. We start with ten cups of ice cream mix, which works out to be five finished pints of each new flavor. All of this is done by hand in the lab, not on the production line in our plant, which is where we make about thirteen million gallons of ice cream a year."

The new ice creams are now tested by another group of fifty consumers. This time, the testers actually get to taste the ice cream, not just read about it. Some people sit in booths, some are in panels, others in classrooms.

On their company's first birthday in 1979, Ben & Jerry celebrated by hosting a "Free Cone Day," a delicious tradition continued each year. In 1999, a half million free ice cream cones were given out in Ben & Jerry's scoop shops all over the US.

The taste tests have strict rules: No talking and no sharing of opinions. Each person will taste a total of four samples—more than four can cause burnout or flavor fatigue—and write an evaluation of the products.

Child taste testers are not hired (although they are often used in the candy and gum industries). That's because kids are not as picky about their ice cream as adults are, and don't have the money to spend on super-premium brands.

There has been one exception to the "no kids" rule, says Kamm.

"We did taste tests with high school and college students for one of our newer flavors, Phish Food, named after a Vermont rock band. It's a sticky, hideously sweet combination of chocolate ice cream, marshmallows, caramel swirls, and fudge fish. Teens love it—it's like eating a whole rich candy bar in every pint!"

Go!

As soon as the prototype testing is finished, the marketing department decides in July which flavors will be developed for commercial sales. After a number of the ice creams have been weeded out, it's time for Kamm's department to head to the plant. From August through October, large test batches—two hundred to six hundred gallons of each flavor—must be made.

Kamm explains why.

"Sometimes, a recipe works fine for a small, single batch of ice cream, but it doesn't translate to bigger batches on bigger equipment in our plant. Our goal is to make the product look and taste the same, no matter how large or small the batch. Often, our engineers must design special equipment to ensure the process works.

"That's what we needed to do with Phish Food. We don't put preservatives in our products, so the marshmallows in that flavor couldn't be made ahead of time. Our engineers developed a special marshmallow whipper that injected the creamy stuff into the ice cream at the last minute. It was a big job, and goes to show you what a fun but complex industry this is . . . and how important a background in science, math, technology—and cooking! —can be."

The marketing department decides in November which flavors will be developed for commercial sales. The ice creams are now ready for another round of taste-testing. If the top five flavors made in the plant get the same approval ratings as the handmade ones—scoring at least an eight on a scale of one to ten—the green light is given for production. Samples of the new flavors roll off the production line and are sent to retailers (grocery stores, supermarkets, scoop shops, etc.) in December and January.

Camel Ice Cream???

Israeli professor Reuven Yagil believes that ice cream made from camel's milk could end the famine that has plagued Africa. "In Kenya, all cattle have died because of the prolonged drought," Yagil said, "but they have a surplus of camel milk." Although the flavor has a slight bitter taste to it—due to the types of plants camels eat—the ice cream is described as tasty and smooth. It is also rich in protein and low in fat. "There is a limit as to how much milk you can drink," Yagil went on, "but you can eat as much of this ice cream as you like."

The Finish Line

April showers bring May . . . ice cream! By the time spring has sprung, five new frozen Ben & Jerry's dessert products are on the shelves for consumers to try.

But Kamm and her coworkers don't have time to stop and celebrate. They've already been busy for three months or more, developing new ice cream flavors for *next* year.

Does Kamm ever get tired of the never-ending cycle?

"The pressure is intense," she admits. "We work against really tight deadlines, so it's challenging and stressful to get things done well *and* fast. And, it's challenging working with such a diverse, passionate group of people. But that's also what's best about this job. We're united in our love of food!"

That food includes the three pints of free ice cream that each Ben & Jerry's employee receives every day!

• 15 •

Cookin' Up Cones: The Joy Cone Company

". . . Lick the scoop slowly so that ice cream melts down the outside of the cone and over your hand . . . Eat a hole in the bottom of the cone and suck the rest of the ice cream out of the bottom. When only the cone remains with ice cream coating the inside, leave on the car dashboard."

—"How to Eat an Ice Cream Cone" from *How to Eat Like a Child* by Delia Ephron, 1977.

The year was 1918.

During the next twelve months, World War I would end . . .

. . . one-quarter of the US population would fall ill in a deadly flu epidemic . . .

. . . Americans would set their clocks ahead to enjoy an extra sunny hour in the first daylight saving time . . .

. . . The popular children's book *Raggedy Ann Stories* would be published . . .

. . . and an immigrant family from Lebanon would bake the soon-to-be-best ice cream cone in the country.

New Jobs in a New World

In the Midwest during the early 1900s, newly arrived immigrants from all over the world labored in steel mills, factories, or foundries. After years of much hard work, many managed to scrape together enough money to start small businesses. The George family from Lebanon was no exception. By scrimping and saving, Albert George, his younger sister, Rose, and her husband, Thomas, proudly opened a small grocery store in Brookfield, Ohio. Albert and Rose invited their mother, Shawneene George, to help them. Shawneene welcomed the change. The hours at the store would be long, but far easier than the back-breaking work she'd done for years as a housecleaner and wash-woman.

One day in 1918, a Lebanese friend of Albert's visited the family. He told them he had worked for a company that baked ice cream cones, and knew where hand-me-down cone-making machines could be bought at a cheap price. The friend made the Georges an offer: If they would hire him as a store clerk, he promised to run the hand-operated equipment and teach them the cone business.

Albert agreed. The family bought the old-fashioned machinery and started selling cones as a sideline. They called their new venture the George and Thomas Cone Company.

The first cones made by Albert and his family were sugar cones. They cooked them on a waffle iron, then rolled them by hand, easy as clay, into a funnel shape while still soft and warm—just as Ernest Hamwi had done years before at the St. Louis World's Fair. Unlike the perfectly molded cones of today, the George's product had a "rough top," meaning a jagged edge around the crown.

The cones sold like hotcakes . . . er, waffles! It wasn't long before the family could afford to modernize their business, phasing out their dated equipment and replacing it with automated machinery.

The new equipment not only helped produce more cones, it also improved the company's image. Hand-rolled cones at this time were considered old-fashioned. In 1913, five years before the Georges had started their cone business, John Grosset, a Swedish engineer, created a cone-molding machine that looked like a miniature Ferris wheel. It baked five thousand cones an hour. He sold the patent to the Consolidated Wafer Company, which proclaimed itself as the "largest manufacturer of Ice Cream Cones in the World." Soon, people were turning up their noses at hand-rolled cones. By 1917, the Consolidated Wafer Company and other manufacturers had begun placing newspaper ads that boasted their cones were "made in clean, sanitary factories from the best materials . . . not made by hand!"

Shawneene George, who for years helped make cones in her children's company, was one of only seven hundred survivors in the 1912 sinking of the RMS Titanic. Fourteen hundred ninety-three people died in the disaster, including three of Shawneene's cousins. Relatives remembered that before Shawneene set sail, her hair was jet-black. Within a year of her catastrophic experience, her hair had dramatically changed to pure white.

Cone of Plenty

The George and Thomas Cone Company—like many small cone manufacturers of that era—continued for several years on an upward spiral of success. There were several reasons for this:

First, at the time, buying ice cream in bulk—meaning, in cartons or containers—was more expensive than buying a single cone. There were a wide variety of machines on the market that could mass-produce molded and waffle cones. But no one had yet invented a machine that could fill a quart or half-gallon container with ice cream quickly, easily, and cheaply. Today, of course, it costs far less to buy a carton of ice cream than to purchase one cone. (Cones sold for 5 cents a piece for almost fifty years. Now, a single scoop can cost you $2.50 or more.) That's because we've made tremendous technological advances in the manufacturing of ice cream—but there is no way to automate the *serving* of ice cream. You must still stand in line, tapping your foot, waiting impatiently for the worker to scoop and serve the dessert.

Second, ice cream cones were popular in the 1920s, '30s, and early '40s because most households did not have refrigerators! The majority of families owned an icebox, which was simply an insulated cabinet, kind of like a large cooler, that held a block of ice. The ice was purchased from an iceman who made daily deliveries to each neighborhood. Food placed in the icebox stayed cool only until the ice melted. People who *could* afford a refrigerator often didn't buy one that had a top freezer section. (The freezers were small, and didn't hold much.) This meant that bulk ice cream stored at home lasted only a few hours before it turned to soup. So a trip to the nearest soda fountain for a

cone was the only way to satisfy a sudden after-dinner ice cream craving.

Third, more and more groceries and drugstores, soda fountains and parlors, were selling ice cream cones, but did not have the equipment to bake their own. So, the cones were in great demand. The George and Thomas Cone Company grew in part because they sold so many cones to the Isaly Dairy, a chain of grocery stores in the Midwest that featured the popular "sky scraper" ice cream cone.

Thousands of small cone-making businesses like Albert's opened in the decade before 1920. The work was easy and could be done by one person. Profits were high, and the start-up costs low: An owner could purchase a six-cone mold and a gasoline stove for under $30. But by the late 1920s, the industry had become almost completely mechanized. Everything from mixing the batter to packing the cones in cases was done by machine. Few could now afford to start their own factories, which cost around $100,000 to open.

To compete in this expensive market, the George family dedicated themselves to baking the best cones in the world—a job they've done now for more than eighty years. Along the way, they changed their name to the Joy Cone Company, after one of their flat-bottomed cones called the Joy cup. Here is their recipe for success.

Best of the Best

Joe George, one of Albert George's sons, is the president of the Joy Cone Company, a job he's held for more than thirty-five years. "Our goal," explains George, "is to make one product better than any other company does. Cones are that product. We have developed our own cone ovens, which are built right here in our plant. The cones are designed by engineers."

So what makes the best cone design?

George counts eight points on his fingers:

1. **A good release from the mold.** Meaning, it must be easy for the machinery to remove the cone from the mold. No sticking, please!

2. **A good baking appearance.** Is the color attractive? Is it even? Or does the cone look pale or half-cooked on one side, too dark or overdone on the other? Does it look appetizing, making you want to fill it immediately with your favorite ice cream and bite into it? "The cone should reflect the light," says George, "and have a shiny—never dull—appearance."

3. **A good even baking throughout.** Does the cone cook evenly? It shouldn't be crispy on one side, soft on the other.

4. **A good strength.** Will it withstand a firm grasp, whether it's the sticky fingers of a toddler or the stronger clutch of a hockey player? Will the cone survive the bumpy journey from the plant to the store without cracking or crumbling? If the cone is prefilled, such as in the case of Drumsticks and other ice cream novelties, "it will need to be strong enough to withstand the punishment that a cone

takes when filled by automatic packing machines," explains Mr. George.

5. **A good portion control.** Will the cone hold a single, double, or triple scoop without breaking?

6. **A good portion appearance.** "This applies to cake or molded cones," George explains. "They should look streamlined, not squat. Also, they should be proportioned so that half the soft-serve is inside the cone, and half outside, atop the cone. If the cone is too narrow in the barrel, you won't get enough inside. If it's too wide, you'll get too much inside, which makes the portions appear smaller."

7. **Efficient packing.** Do the cones nest well inside one another to save space during storage and delivery? Do they need a minimum amount of packing material to keep them from breaking?

8. Last but not least: the cones must have a **good taste.** "They should have a mild, pleasant cereal taste," says George. A good cone should complement the ice cream, not overwhelm it with a strong flavor.

Zzzzzzzz

It's 3 A.M. in Hermitage, Pennsylvania. Everyone in town is fast asleep . . . everyone, that is, except the night-shift workers at the Joy Cone Company. To meet demand, "we run our plant twenty-four hours a day, seven days a week," says George, "although we always shut down for holidays."

George then goes on to explain how the cones are made at his plant.

"The first step," he says, "is to mix the batter. There are

three main ingredients: sugar, wheat flour, and tapioca flour."

Wait a minute . . . tapioca? Isn't that a pudding?

Yes, but flour is also made from tapioca, the starchy root of the tropical cassava plant. Tapioca is used to add strength to the cones.

Joy Cone's tapioca flour is flown in all the way from Thailand. Then it's delivered by truck, packed in hundred-pound bags. The sugar is also shipped by truck, in tote bags that weigh as much as a rhinoceros: two thousand pounds! The wheat flour arrives in big tank trailers, and is blown with compressors into silos.

"We have three silos that are seventy feet tall," says George. "Each holds one hundred sixty thousand pounds of flour."

The entire plant—all two hundred thousand square feet of it—is run electronically, by computer, including the refrigerated coolers where the batter is stored.

"When a cooler runs low on batter," George explains, "a batter-level indicator is tripped, which sends a signal to one of two mixers. [Sugar- and cake-cone batters are

In the 1930s the National Biscuit Company designed the Jack and Jill, the Siamese twins of cone molds, which held two scoops of ice cream side by side. During World War II, cone manufacturers had difficulty obtaining wheat flour, since it was needed to make bread and other food products for American soldiers overseas. Several companies in Philadelphia solved this problem by making ice cream cones out of crushed, sweetened popcorn!

made in different mixers.] The signal tells the mixer two things: one, that the batter is low; and two, in which cooler the batter is low.

"Signals are also sent to the wheat flour, tapioca flour, and sugar storage areas so that correct amounts are blown into the mixer. Other signals control the portion of water coming into the mixer, and turn the mixer on. Our cake-cone mixer produces about three hundred pounds of batter at a time; our sugar-cone mixer does about half that.

"After the batter has mixed for nine minutes, another signal in the production area notifies an attendant that it is time to come back into the batter room. She will check the batter to make sure everything is okay. If it is, she will add the remaining ingredients by hand." These ingredients include: shortening (a type of edible grease or fat that makes baked goods crisp), baking powder (that makes the dough rise), flavoring, natural food coloring, and salt.

The mixer is then reset by the attendant. It will beat the batter at a high speed for a short time. Then—ding!—the mixer shuts off automatically. The batter is pumped into the cooler, ready for a new batch of cones. The mixer resets itself so it will be ready for the next cooler that runs low on batter.

Hot stuff

George leads the way to another section of the plant. This is where the baking machines will produce five million cones per day—or about one billion cones a year! Here's what happens next:

"The batter is now pumped automatically from the cooler to a tank inside one of our forty baking ovens," says

Joy Cone Company makes three distinct types of cones: sugar cones, waffle cones, and cake or molded cones. Sugar and waffle cones are cooked like a flat waffle, then rolled to form a funnel or horn shape. The batter is more than one-third sugar and creates a strong texture for prefilling and packing. For cake cones, less than 5 percent sugar is used. The batter is poured into a mold, and the cone is pressed, coming out of the oven in its finished shape. Take a peek inside an empty molded cone. Do you notice a ledge and a ring of "teeth?" The teeth in the flared or bell-shaped top were designed to give cones more strength. The ledge serves as a drip ring, helping to keep melting ice cream inside the cone—not dripping all over you!

George. "From there, it takes another little ride through a pipe, pumping into either the cake-cone molds or the sugar-cone plates. Each mold or plate receives a premeasured amount of batter."

How long does it take to bake a cone?

"About ninety seconds for a cake cone," George estimates. "Sugar and waffle cones a little less: eighty-two seconds. But then it takes twenty seconds for our machines to wind them into a cone shape, and two minutes to air-cool." Sugar and waffle cones are still soft and warm when they're rolled, so they must be completely cooled before packing—otherwise, they lose their shape. Cake cones can be packed as soon as they're baked because they come out of the oven already crisp and molded.

Are any cones ever damaged or rejected?

"Oh, yes, occasionally," George goes on. "Our production people are responsible for quality control. This means they watch the cones, taste them periodically, and set aside samples for a more thorough examination. They'll reject any cones that are broken or incomplete. Less frequently, cones may be rejected if they're under- or overbaked. Rejected cones are ground up and sold for animal feed."

Harold Schuchardt, whose parents ran a small cone-baking company in Wisconsin in the 1920s, remembers his boyhood days, when broken cones were the rule, not the exception.

"We bagged and sold broken or defective cones to the neighbors for five cents," Mr. Schuchardt reminisced. "There was no television, so families sat on their front porches on hot summer evenings, enjoying these treats. Mothers would grind up pieces of the broken cones and use them instead of nuts on desserts."

Of course, that was more than seventy years ago, when immaculate, air-conditioned, efficient, and completely automated plants like the Joy Cone Company were only a dream of the future. Mr. Schuchardt recalls helping his parents (who later made chocolate-covered Drumstick cones for the Eskimo Pie Corporation) bake the waffle cones in a small room with temperatures rising to over 100 stifling degrees.

> **"The ice cream cone is the only ecologically sound package. It is the perfect package."**
>
> Comment made by a Health, Education and Welfare (HEW) official on a 1969 broadcast of the TV show *Sixty Minutes*

"We stirred the batter by hand in a vat, and constantly wiped the hot plates [waffle irons] with a cloth covered in cooking oil," he said. "We used insulated gloves and an ice pick to remove the cones from the plates, wrapping them around cone-shaped wooden dowels until they cooled. It took a lot of work . . . and sometimes we were still at it at nine o'clock at night, after our hired help had gone for the day."

Beep-Beep!

Once the cones have cooled completely, another automated journey will take them through the packing machines, where they will be boxed in protective packaging. Since sugar and waffle cones are more fragile than cake cones, they are packed in what George calls a "foam clamshell type of container" to help cushion them from breakage. Then the packaged cones are loaded into trucks for shipping.

George emphasizes the importance of getting the cones to market quickly and efficiently. Although the shelf life—how long a cone will stay

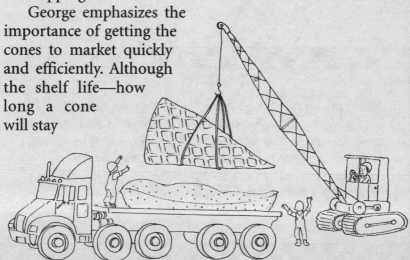

fresh—is more than a year, the ideal time between baking and eating is two months. "That's why we own and operate our own fleet of trucks in the Eastern United States," he says with pride. "It ensures that our cones are handled properly from the time they leave the plant until they arrive at their destination. Our trucks are equipped with air-ride suspensions in both the tractors and the trailers." This gives the cones—and the drivers!—a fast, smooth ride.

For now, Joy Cone must use an outside trucking service to ship cones to the West Coast. But they plan to open another plant soon in Flagstaff, Arizona. Then they can run their own trucks out of this plant to service customers in the Western US.

The trucks aren't cheap, and it costs more to ship cones this way. But the company believes the results are worth it. Joy Cone has a "reliable delivery system and almost no breakage."

All ice cream cones had pointy bottoms until the late 1940s. That's when Joseph Shapiro of the Maryland Cup Corporation (now the Ace Baking Company) invented the first flat-bottom cone. He designed it especially for the Dairy Queen restaurants. The DQ workers loved the cones because they could stand them on the counter while filling orders.

Ice Cream Day

So now the cones are speeding on their way.

But where do they go?

"There are three main sales areas—meaning customers—for the marketing of ice cream cones," says George.

"The first is called the Dairy Pack Industry. These are sugar cones we sell to dairies. The cones are prefilled there with ice cream, then frozen and sold as ice cream novelties. Two brand names you might be familiar with are Drumstick and Nutty Buddy.

"**The World's Largest Ice Cream Cone**" was actually a balloon. The forty-four-foot-high, sixteen-foot-wide, triple-scoop, helium-filled "cone" floated above the crowd in the 1945 Macy's Thanksgiving Parade.

"The second area is called the Retail Trade. These are cones sold to supermarkets and convenience stores.

"The third area is known in our business as Food Service. We supply restaurants, such as Dairy Queen, McDonald's, Hardee's, and Friendly's, with our products. We also sell to amusement parks."

And, of course, there are always plenty of cones on hand for Ice Cream Day.

Every Thursday afternoon at the Pennsylvania plant, free ice cream cones are handed out to employees and neighborhood kids. It's a tradition the company has continued for many years.

"Tradition is the glue that keeps the family together," adds Mr. George. "We are a family business. But our employees—and the local children—are a part of that family."

So the next time you find yourself strolling down Lamor Road in Hermitage, Pennsylvania, on a Thursday afternoon, stop in for a taste of tradition and a scoop of joy . . . courtesy of the Joy Cone Company.

"An ice cream cone can solve any problem—even if it's only for a few minutes."

—anonymous

Ice Cream Scream
by Joan Bransfield Graham

CHERRY
vanilla
is calling to
me with its ruby
promises as my lips
slip toward that
chocolate-chipped
rocky road;
there
are no STOP
signs, only GO GO
pistachio and I'm
in a strawberry
hurry to budge the fudge.

SUGAR CONE

WAFFLE

CONE

ONE

ON

O

Section 6

SCOOP IT UP!

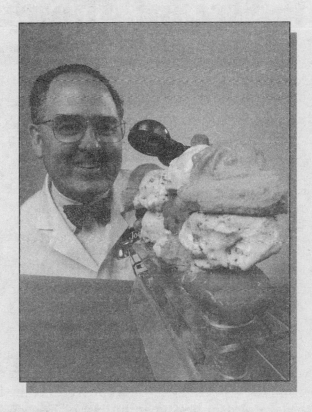

John Harrison, official taste tester for Dreyer's Grand Ice Cream, recommends that you allow ice cream to warm up for five minutes or so before serving. A warmer temperature brings out a fuller flavor. The ice cream is also easier to scoop!

Photo credit: Courtesy Dreyer's Grand Ice Cream

Something to Scream About: Famous Ice Cream Companies

Crime ace Eric Mace
Had evidence on his face.
What it was, no one knew,
Till Eric offered up a clue:
"Take the first line
of this rhyme,
Unscramble it in double time.
Unlike me, I predict
You'll have this sticky case well-licked!"

—"Scooper Sleuth" by Fred Borchers

On a scorching summer day, when the sun soars high and you need a cooling treat, which brand of ice cream makes you scream the loudest? Are you a cone-crunching fan of Dairy Queen? A drip-licking enthusiast of Häagen-Dazs? Do you crave a cup brimming with Baskin-Robbins' 31-derful flavors? Or are you a loyal advocate of that other dynamic duo, Ben & Jerry?

To help you choose, try a tasty sampling of just a few

of the popular national brands that are worth ice-screaming about . . .

"ALL NATURAL": BREYERS ICE CREAM

1866: The American Civil War had ended the year before. Yet the country still faced another battle: that of slowly recovering from the wounds of painful memories and losses.

William Breyer knew that people needed a treat now more than ever. So he dusted off his old hand-crank freezer, made a batch of ice cream in his small kitchen, and sold it to his friends and neighbors in Philadelphia, Pennsylvania.

The dessert was a welcome and instant hit. Neighbors loved the taste of Breyer's ice cream, which he pledged was made with only the finest natural ingredients. To meet the increasing demand, Breyer hitched his white horse, Old Peacock, to a wagon, and began clip-clopping along the city streets every day, delivering his ice cream door-to-door, announcing his arrival with an old bell.

Sixteen years of sweet success later, Breyer opened his first retail ice cream store; four more opened not long after. Still, Breyer and his family continued to make all the ice cream the old-fashioned way, hand-cranking each batch and delivering it by wagon. He and Old Peacock became well-known sights among the city dwellers as they continued their rounds, day after day.

After Breyer's death, his son, Henry, opened a whole-sale manufacturing plant, which was producing over a million gallons of ice cream a year by 1918. The ice cream was bought by confectionaries and soda fountains throughout New York, New Jersey, and Washington, DC.

To honor his father, Henry added Breyer's "Pledge of Purity" to every package. That promise still holds today: the Good Humor-Breyer's company guarantees that each container of its twenty delicious flavors is filled with "the best ice cream available, while remaining pure and all-natural." This commitment to quality has helped Breyer's to become the #1 brand of ice cream in America.

THE GRAND DESSERT OF GRAND AVENUE: DREYER'S/EDY'S GRAND ICE CREAM

The *SS Kaiser Wilhelm* steamed away from its German port in the fall of 1906, on a luxury cruise bound for America. On the last night of the voyage, one of the galley boys, eighteen-year-old William Dreyer, was rewarded for a job well-done during the journey. His prize? The honor of making a frozen dessert for the captain's table. Thinking quickly, Dreyer gathered together the fresh fruit, sugar, and other ingredients needed to make a delicious water ice. The captain and his officers sent their highest compliments to the chef. Dreyer was thrilled, and that very night he decided to pursue a life in ice cream.

After apprenticing for many years with some of the best ice cream makers in the country, Dreyer started his own creamery and ice cream factory in northern California. He then linked up with Joe Edy, an expert confectioner who owned six candy parlors in the San Francisco Bay area. The two men formed a partnership, opening Edy's Grand Ice Cream in 1928. The name had a double meaning: the original factory debuted on Grand Avenue in Oakland, California, and the partners wanted to declare "the magnificence of their ice cream."

The following year Dreyer and Edy created what would become their most famous ice cream of all time.

It was the fall of 1929, only weeks after the stock-market crash that would plunge America into the Great Depression. The partners produced a new taste sensation by putting chopped almonds and marshmallow bits—which they had to snip into bite-size pieces using their wives' sewing scissors—into chocolate ice cream. "They knew tough times were just around the corner," explains John Harrison, Dreyer's official taste tester, "so Dreyer and Edy hoped the flavor name would at least give people something to smile about." The amusing name they chose? Rocky Road!

During the next eighteen years, Dreyer was in charge of making the premium products; Edy used his confectionary expertise to create fancy ice cream cakes, logs, molds, and other decorative desserts. The ice cream sold well, and the Grand Avenue store was a hub of happy customers, from teens to housewives to the social elite.

In July of 1947, Edy chose to disband the partnership, wanting to pursue his first sweet love: candy. He went on to open more confection shops and a factory in the Los Angeles area, while Dreyer went solo, creating a brand-new "state-of-the-art ice cream plant." He rechristened his company Dreyer's Grand Ice Cream, although the product is still known today as Edy's in the Midwest and East Coast—a nod of thanks for Edy's delicious contributions.

Ninety years after the wide-eyed galley boy set foot for the first time in America, the company he started would become the leading manufacturer, marketer and distributor of premium ice cream in the US. Today it boasts five manufacturing sites—including a Fort Wayne, Indiana, factory, the largest packaged ice cream plant in the world—with twenty-four hundred employees, and yearly earnings of $796 million dollars.

And, of course, a continued "grand" future!

THE ICE CREAM WITH THE BRIGHT ORANGE ROOF: HOWARD JOHNSON'S

"Say, what did you think of that ice cream?" Howard Johnson asked his first customer. "Be just great," the customer replied, "if you could get the sand out of it!"

After returning to the States at the end of World War I, the young, newly discharged soldier, Howard Johnson, had opened a drugstore/soda fountain in his hometown of Wollaston, Massachusetts. Disliking the artificial-tasting ice cream he bought from a local distributor, Johnson hired an expert from Boston to teach him the tricks of the ice cream trade. His first batch was a gritty disaster, but Johnson persevered, experimenting with recipes every night in the basement of his shop. He knew if the ice cream was going to bear his name, it would have to be the best-tasting ever. Soon, he'd perfected twenty-eight recipes, which he kept safe in a secret notebook he shared with only one assistant.

"Before long," he recalled, "people crowded into that [ten-seat] shop. They formed lines down the block. . . I would [make] cones so big . . . that the kids had to use two hands to hold them. Somebody once looked at that ice cream cone and figured it was costing me eight-and-a-half cents—and I sold it for a dime. Not what you'd call a great profit, but it made me . . . and that ice cream, famous."

Soon after, Johnson opened a small ice cream stand at nearby Wollaston Beach. He painted the roof an eye-catching orange, and people flocked to try his finger-lickin' good cones.

Johnson owned no delivery truck, so he had to ferry drumsful of ice cream to the beach in taxicabs. "We kept running out," Johnson said, "and I'd send back to town for more and call out to the crowd: *'Stand by, everybody! More ice cream on the way!'* The crowds grew so large, twelve policemen were needed to keep people from becoming unruly. On one especially hot August afternoon, Johnson scooped a record fourteen thousand cones. To meet the demand, Johnson kept his ten ice cream freezers running twenty-one hours a day.

In the early 1930s, Johnson opened a chain of orange-roofed ice cream stands along numerous beaches and roads in Massachusetts. The first Howard Johnson's restaurant was franchised in 1935. Five years later, there were 130 of them across the Northeast; by 1971, the company boasted nine hundred restaurants, four hundred motor lodges, and thousands of employees from the Atlantic to the Pacific. Weary or hungry travelers loved to stop at Howard Johnson's—and still do. The motels and restaurants are a safe guarantee: they are clean, kid-friendly, and always serve up good food, good service, and delicious ice cream.

THE CONE WITH THE CURL ON TOP:
DAIRY QUEEN

The sign in the Kankakee, Illinois, ice cream shop read: "All the ice cream you can eat for only 10 cents." A crowd of waiting people snaked up and down the block and around the corner. Within two hours, J.F. "Grandpa" McCullough and his son Alex had hand-dipped sixteen hundred cups of the new frozen treat. They'd planned the special sale that August day in 1938 to see if customers would like their invention: the first soft-serve ice cream.

The experiment was a lip-smacking success, and a "royal" dessert was born: Dairy Queen.

For many years, Grandpa and Alex had owned and operated the Homemade Ice Cream Company. The McCulloughs made ice cream in the 1930s using a batch freezer, filling three-gallon tubs with the semisoft dessert, then placing them in a deep freeze to harden at –10 degrees F. But Grandpa had always preferred the taste of ice cream as it oozed soft and fresh from the batch freezer spigot. The dessert was a delicious 23 degrees F, which didn't numb the taste buds. "Wouldn't it be great," he thought one day, "if there were a freezer that could dispense semifrozen ice cream that still held its shape?"

One-third of American households eat at least one gallon of ice cream and related frozen desserts every two weeks.

He'd seen an ad for a continuous freezer that produced frozen custard. Perhaps something similar could be created for his unique ice cream.

It took Grandpa and Alex two years, working with an inventor and a dairy manufacturing company, to design and produce the first soft-serve freezer/dispenser. Meanwhile, they also worked to perfect the recipe for their new treat. On June 22, 1940, the McCulloughs opened the Dairy Queen doors and spigots in Joliet, Illinois. Two more stores had opened by December 1941.

Then the Japanese bombed Pearl Harbor, and the US plunged into World War II. Ice cream was classified by our government as a "nonessential" food. This mean that ice cream production would slow from a steady stream to a drip.

The National Dairy Council and the International Association of Ice Cream Manufacturers jumped into action. Ice cream was wholesome and healthful, they argued. And, studies proved that eating ice cream raised morale among soldiers overseas and their families waiting back home. It was also noted that doctors often prescribed ice cream to help soldiers recover from psychological wounds.

Within months the government had relented. Ice cream was reclassified, and placed on a Basic Seven Foods Chart. Manufacturers could start producing the dessert again, but sugar and vanilla rationing still made ice cream a luxury. This kept the McCulloughs from expanding their shops; the stores still in operation were closed at least one week out of every month when ingredients grew low. One franchisee recalled running "out of soft-serve with two long lines of customers standing in front of us." Many restaurants stopped serving ice cream altogether, specializing instead in sherbets. One confectioner took to advertising cottage cheese sundaes—but stopped when no one would eat them.

When the war and rationing finally ended in 1945, Dairy Queen immediately opened five new stores, and had a total of one hundred of them in a booming business by 1947. The "cone with the curl on top" was an American Institution by 1950, with fourteen hundred stores open across the country. They also paved the road for the debut of other soft-serve ice cream companies, such as the popular Tastee-Freez, Carvel Dari-Freeze, and Foster's Freeze.

Today, the dessert is swirled into curls atop cones and in cups in more than six thousand franchise stores around the world.

And the ice cream's regal name? Grandpa chose it because "he believed his soft-serve was the 'queen' among dairy products, the epitome of freshness and wholesomeness." Millions of kids agree!

31-DERFUL FLAVORS:
BASKIN-ROBBINS

They were brothers-in-law and ice cream rivals. Irving "Irv" Robbins owned the Snowbird Ice Cream Store on one end of the city; across town, Burton "Burt" Baskin was the proprietor of Burton's Ice Cream Parlor. But in 1946 they ended their competitive ways, and formed a delicious partnership in Glendale, California: Baskin-Robbins.

For many years after World War II, good ice cream fell on hard times. Soda fountains dried up. Home freezer sales slacked off. The reason: Grocery stores and supermarkets were mass-producing their own products, which were cheaply made and cheaply priced. (A half gallon sold for only 69 cents.) Containing low quantities of butterfat and high quantities of air, the ice cream was bland and lacking in richness. The super-

To help improve the morale of soldiers serving in the South Pacific during World War II, the US Navy spent one million dollars to build a huge floating ice cream parlor near the island of Guadalcanal.

market brands sold well anyway—at least for a while—since just about anyone could now afford to take a carton home. This forced the higher-quality ice cream companies and factories out of business. Between 1957 and 1969, almost seventeen hundred ice cream plants across the country closed their doors forever. Overall sales dipped dramatically in the 1950s.

Baskin-Robbins helped to halt the decline in ice cream's quality and sales by introducing premium ice cream in premium flavors: 31 of them . . . one for every day of the month.

The rich ice cream from the "olden days" caught on again, and Baskin-Robbins experimented with more exotic taste sensations, eventually inventing seven hundred in all. They specialized in creating *fun* flavors—with names to match—that focused on major American events. When the Beatles arrived from England for their first US tour in 1964, Baskin-Robbins celebrated by introducing "Beatlenut" ice cream. When millions flocked to see Sean Connery star as the dashing 007 in a 1965 James Bond film, Baskin-Robbins offered their "0031 Secret Bonded Flavor." In 1969, when Neil Armstrong stepped onto the moon in one giant leap for mankind, Baskin-Robbins offered one giant scoop back home with their "Lunar Cheesecake" ice cream.

Their most famous flavor of all, however, was inspired when Irv stumbled upon toffee-coated pecans on a trip to New Orleans in 1970. He thought the pecans were scrumptious, and believed they'd be even more tasty if sprinkled into vanilla ice cream. Back at work, he added a ribbon of caramel to the concoction, creating Pralines 'N Cream. Within two months of introducing this creamy flavor, Baskin-Robbins would be the only ice cream store in the world to feature a flavor that consistently outsells vanilla.

Not all of Baskin-Robbins's flavors have received delicious reviews. Their "Goody-Goody Gum Drop" ice cream was dropped from the flavor lists not long after its invention because the gumdrops froze as hard as rocks—putting customers at risk for cracked teeth. A ketchup-flavored ice cream, made for a friend who loved to splurt the stuff on everything, crashed and burned in one day at the Baskin-Robbins Encino, California, store, where everyone hated it—including the ketchup fan.

Today, Baskin-Robbins is the largest manufacturer of premium ice cream products, and the largest chain of ice cream speciality stores. There are almost four thousand of the franchised outlets in fifty-seven countries around the world, including Russia, India, Saudi Arabia, and Australia.

THE CRÈME DE LA CRÈME OF ICE CREAMS: HÄAGEN-DAZS

The name sounded Danish, but in Denmark the words were gibberish. The *umlaut* looked impressive, but Danes had never seen that double-dot mark in their language. In fact, the company founder hailed from the Bronx—by way of Poland—and it was his wife who invented the nonsensical name. But today, Häagen-Dazs translates into the world's leading brand of superpremium ice cream.

As a boy, Reuben Mattus immigrated to New York from Poland with his mother and siblings after his father was killed during World War I. To make money in their new country, the family sold lemon ices and ice cream from a horse-drawn wagon along the streets of the Bronx. As an adult, Mattus tried to stay in the ice cream business. But the boom in supermarket sales squeezed him out of the market. He finally realized that he couldn't compete without risking financial ruin.

But he didn't hang up his scoops.

Instead, Mattus came up with an ingenious plan. "I thought," he said, "that if I made the very best ice cream, people would be willing to pay for it." So in 1961, he set about developing a *superpremium* ice cream, one made from all natural ingredients. (Premium contains at least 12 percent butterfat; superpremium has at least 14 percent.) The result was rich, dense, delectable—and outrageously expensive, costing twice as much as any supermarket brand of ice cream.

Since Denmark was a country with a good image, Mattus's wife, Rose, bestowed the new product with a

Danish-sounding, highbrow name. The snooty moniker got customer attention, but it was the ice cream that won people over. The treat soon became the ice cream of gourmets, and a status symbol for the rich and famous. It was the fastest-growing ice cream company of the 1960s, '70s and '80s, helping to pave a cool, smooth path for other superpremium brands, such as Ben & Jerry's, to enter the market.

Today, Häagen-Dazs (owned by Pillsbury) sells its frozen desserts—including ice cream, yogurt, sorbets, and novelties—in 850 dipping shops in twenty-eight countries. Many still consider it the crème de la crème of ice creams.

Answer to "Scooper Sleuth" riddle: "Ice Cream"

• 17 •

Mmm-mm, Good!: Ice Cream Recipes

Crack the egg
Against the edge.
Add the sweet . . . to make a treat.
Pour in cream
With summer's dream
And turn, turn . . . turn the churn.
The sound is nice
As salt and ice
Go 'round, 'round . . . 'round and 'round.
We have to turn
Until the churn
Goes slower, slow . . . and then won't go.
And when we eat
Our hard-earned treat,
Winter's ice . . . tastes twice as nice!

—"Homemade Ice Cream" by Marni McGee

Ice Cream in a Bag

Kids ages two to 102 can make this ice cream with little muss or fuss—and it's delicious! You don't need an ice cream machine, and you don't need a freezer for hardening or storage, so you can make this recipe on camping trips, at parties, school, the beach—just about anywhere!

Equipment needed:
    1 Ziploc brand sandwich bag, or other sandwich-size plastic sealable bag
    1 Ziploc brand freezer bag (quart-sized), or other large, plastic sealable freezer bag
    Pair of oven mitts
    Dish towel
    Spoon

Ingredients needed:
    1/2 cup heavy whipping cream
    1 tablespoon sugar
    1/4 teaspoon vanilla extract
    2 cups ice cubes (about two large handfuls)
    6 tablespoons rock salt

Directions:
1. Pour the cream into the sandwich-sized bag.
2. Add sugar and vanilla extract to the same bag.
3. Seal the bag. (Make sure it's tightly closed, otherwise your ingredients will leak.)
4. Place the closed sandwich bag inside the freezer bag.
5. Pour the ice into the freezer bag.
6. Pour the rock salt into the freezer bag.
7. Seal the freezer bag. Tightly, please!

8. Put on your oven mitts; or wrap the dish towel loosely around the freezer bag.
9. Shake, rock, roll, and squeeze the bag for a full 5 minutes. (Note: the bag is going to get very cold, 18-20 degrees F. The mitts or dish towel will keep your hands from freezing.)
10. Open the freezer bag and remove the sandwich bag. Using the dish towel, quickly wipe away any rock salt and water from the outside of the sandwich bag. (The ice will have almost completely melted, so the outside of your sandwich bag will be wet.) This will keep the salt and water out of your sandwich bag—and your ice cream!—when you open it.
11. Open the sandwich bag and . . . enjoy! You may eat the ice cream right out of the bag, or spoon it into a bowl. To remove every last delicious bit of the ice cream, turn the bag inside out and scrape the sides with your spoon.

●MAKES 1 SERVING.

Serving suggestions: Try drizzling chocolate sauce or other syrups atop your ice cream . . . sprinkling chocolate chips, jimmies, M&M's, granola, or nuts over it . . . or mixing it with fresh strawberries, raspberries, blueberries, or peaches.

Doc Wilson's Classic Vanilla Ice Cream

According to the International Ice Cream Association, vanilla is the most popular ice cream flavor in the country. It is also the base mix needed for making all other flavors. Once you've learned how to make a good

"It looks like ice cream. Vanilla."—comment made by a 10-year-old New York girl on December 25, 1998, after seeing the first Christmas snow in Central Park in more than twenty years.

vanilla, then you can experiment with recipes for chocolate, strawberry . . . even pickle ice cream!

The following recipe is from the files of Steve "Doc" Wilson. The ice cream is easy, creamy, and delicious. Just what the doctor ordered!

Equipment needed:
Large mixing bowl
Can opener
Whisk
Measuring spoons
Large wooden spoon
Ice cream freezer (hand-crank or electric)

Ingredients needed:
2 large fresh eggs
1 14-ounce can sweetened condensed milk
1 quart heavy whipping cream
1 pint Half & Half cream
1/4 teaspoon salt
2 tablespoons vanilla extract
Rock salt and ice (Read the directions that came with your ice cream freezer to see how much you will need.)

Directions:

1. In the large bowl, whisk—do not beat!—the eggs until slightly blended.
2. Open the can of condensed milk and add to the eggs.
3. Whisk together till blended.
4. Add the heavy whipping cream and Half & Half. Mix well with the wooden spoon.
5. Add salt and vanilla extract. Stir until blended.
6. Pour the mixture into the canister that comes with your ice cream freezer. Cover and chill in your refrigerator for *at least* four hours.
7. Now follow the directions that came with your ice cream freezer for making ice cream. (Most freezers take 20–40 minutes to churn the ice cream.)
8. For soft ice cream, serve and eat immediately. For best flavor and texture, harden the ice cream either in the ice cream freezer (follow manufacturer's instructions) or in your refrigerator's freezer for 3–4 hours.

● MAKES 1 1/2–2 QUARTS OF ICE CREAM.

TIPS:
- Always use real vanilla extract, not imitation, for the best flavor.
- Crushed ice works faster and better than ice cubes, but either may be used.
- Regular table salt may be substituted for rock salt in a . . . um, pinch! Keep in mind, though, that you will need twice as much, and that table salt is far more expensive than rock salt. Read the directions that come with your ice cream freezer to make sure you can use table salt with it. Some freezer mechanisms may become damaged from the tiny salt granules.

- Allow plenty of time for making the ice cream. For example, if you're having a late-afternoon or evening party, start preparing the ice cream early that morning or the night before. This will give the ice cream plenty of time to age and harden.
- If you want to harden your ice cream in your refrigerator's freezer, remove the ice cream from its canister and repack it in a plastic container (such as Tupperware). Cover and freeze. The container should be round, not square. (Round containers offer better air flow for freezing.) Never pack or press hard on the ice cream when switching it to another container. This squishes out the air, and ruins the smooth, creamy texture.
- Always use a rubber spatula to remove the ice cream from its canister. If you use a metal spoon or spatula, you could accidentally dent the metal container. This could cause leaks or prevent the canister from turning smoothly during the freezing process.
- If you don't eat all your homemade ice cream at once, place it in a plastic container, such as Tupperware, cover it, and place in your freezer. Eat within one or two days.

"Ice Cream Soup"
Syrup and ice cream, 'round and 'round
Softening the line between white and brown
Melting tigers into swirling tan
Making ice cream soup last as long as I can!

—April Halprin Wayland

E-Z Hot Fudge Sauce

Equipment needed:
Medium-size sauce pan
Measuring spoons
Measuring cups
Whisk
Wooden spoon

Ingredients needed:
2/3 cup heavy whipping cream
2 tablespoons light corn syrup
12 ounces semisweet chocolate chips

Important: You will be working with a hot stove, so please have an adult present when making this sauce.

Directions:
1. Pour cream and corn syrup into the saucepan.
2. Heat slowly, on medium-low, stirring constantly with the wooden spoon, just till the sauce begins to bubble.
3. Remove from heat. (Don't forget to turn off the stove!)
4. Add the chocolate chips.
5. Whisk until the chips have melted and the sauce is smooth.
6. Pour immediately over ice cream and serve.
7. If you have sauce left over, you may pour it into a plastic container, cover, and keep in your refrigerator for up to three days.
8. To rewarm the sauce, spoon it into a sauce pan. Heat on low, stirring constantly, until the sauce is lukewarm.

● MAKES 2 CUPS.

Homemade Ice Cream Cones

Equipment needed:
Mixing bowl
8-inch, nonstick skillet
Measuring cups
Measuring spoons
Wide rubber spatula
Wooden spoon
Paper towels
Toothpicks

Ingredients needed:
2/3 cup flour
1/4 cup sugar
1/4 cup cooking oil
3 tablespoons water
2 egg whites
1 teaspoon vanilla extract
1 can nonstick cooking spray

Important: You will be working with a hot stove, so please have an adult present before making these cones.

Directions:
1. Spray skillet with nonstick cooking spray.
2. On stove, preheat skillet on medium-low heat.
3. Separate the egg whites. Throw away the shells; if possible, save the yolks for another use.
4. In the mixing bowl, stir together the flour and sugar.
5. Next, add the oil, water, egg whites, and vanilla. Stir until smooth. (The batter will be thick and creamy-looking.)

6. Pour two tablespoons of the batter into the skillet.
7. Using the wooden spoon, spread the batter into a thin circle, about five inches in diameter. (It will look like a big, thin pancake.)
8. Cook until light brown. (About three minutes.)
9. Flip the "pancake" using the rubber spatula. Cook until brown, another minute or two.
10. Using the spatula, remove the soft "pancake" from the pan and place on a paper towel. Quickly, roll it into the shape of a cone. (Watch your fingers—it's hot!) Close the edge with a toothpick.
11. Cool the cone for about five minutes, toothpick side down. The soft cone will get crispier as it cools.
12. Repeat with the rest of the batter.

Serve immediately with ice cream and your favorite toppings. (You may store the cones for twenty-four hours in a tightly covered container, but they will lose their crispness.)

● MAKES ABOUT 8 CONES.

Eating the Ice Cream Cone

If the occasion should arise when a Gentlewoman is offered an ice cream cone, she should refrain from eating it in a public place. Exposure of the tongue by using its tip to lick the ice cream from the cone will serve only to mark her as a woman of unsavory and unattractive appetites. The Gentlewoman should take the ice cream cone home, place it upside down in a shallow dish, discard the cone and eat the ice cream with a spoon.

—advice from an anonymous nineteenth-century source.

Ice Cream Soda

In a long, tall glass, pour about 3 ounces of seltzer or plain soda water. Add about 3 ounces of your favorite syrup. Stir with a long spoon. Add 3 ounces of milk. Stir. Plop in 2 scoops of ice cream (any flavor). Add 6 more ounces of seltzer. Stir slowly so as not to cause an overflow. Add a drop or two more of syrup for extra flavor. Top with a dollop of whipped cream. Serve.

TO MARKET, TO MARKET: ICE CREAM SHOPPING TIPS

- To keep your ice cream from melting, get all the other items on your grocery list first. Put ice cream into your cart only when you're ready to pay and leave the store.
- Choose a carton that is as far back in the freezer as possible. Make sure it is rock hard. If the carton is soft or squishy to the touch, don't buy it. This means it has partially melted. Take it to the store manager or check-out person, and choose another carton.
- If the ice cream you want is stored in an open top freezer case, always choose a carton or box that sits below the freezer line.
- Ask to have the ice cream double-bagged in a brown paper bag—never plastic!—to help keep the carton cold. (Brown paper bags are good insulators.) If you're buying several cartons at once, place them all in the same bag.
- If you want your ice cream to stay as cold as possible on the ride home, place it inside an ice chest, cooler, or thermal bag filled with ice or ice packs.

- Take your ice cream home immediately. If you make any stops along the way, you could end up with an ice cream puddle—or worse. Ice cream that has partially melted and then been refrozen will taste terrible and have a sandy texture.

The world's largest "black cow" (root beer float) was made on May 18, 1996, by the Thomas Kemper Soda Company of Seattle, Washington. The float contained 166 gallons of root beer; 500 people were needed to drink it.

COOL IT!
TIPS FOR KEEPING YOUR ICE CREAM FRESH AND COLD

- Unpack your ice cream and put it in the freezer as soon as you get home.
- The best place to store ice cream and frozen novelties is in a deep freeze. (Ice Cream stays its freshest and hardest if kept at 10–20 degrees below zero.) You can keep ice cream in a deep freeze for up to three months, as long as you don't open and shut the door too often.
- If storing ice cream in the regular freezer compartment of your refrigerator, place the containcrs sidc by side, on the bottom shelf, pushed as far back as possible. Never place them on the top shelf or on the door. (Heat rises, so the bottom shelf is the coolest place in your freezer.)

- Eat store-bought ice cream within seven days of purchasing it. For best flavor and texture, eat the ice cream within two or three days—especially if you have a self-defrosting freezer. (Homemade ice cream should be eaten within twenty-four hours.) These units run on alternating defrost/freeze cycles, which means they warm up enough to rid the walls of ice, then quickly chill everything again. This doesn't harm most frozen foods, such as vegetables or hamburger, but it does harm processed foods, causing freezer burn (an old or papery flavor) or ice crystals in your ice cream.
- After scooping some ice cream out of the container, lay a piece of plastic wrap or waxed paper across the top of the container before replacing the lid. This will help keep air out of the ice cream, and stop ice crystals from forming.
- Put the ice cream container away immediately after serving. Never allow it to sit on the counter while you eat your dessert.
- Never store uncovered foods in your freezer; their odors can affect the taste of your ice cream.

SCOOP IT UP:
ICE CREAM SERVING SUGGESTIONS

- Allow ice cream to warm up for five minutes or so before serving. A warmer temperature brings out a fuller flavor. It's also easier to scoop.
(Note: chocolate ice cream melts faster than vanilla, so you may want to serve it at a lower temperature.)
- Always use an ice cream dipper or scoop, not a spoon, to get nicely rounded portions. (A standard #24 scoop is about two inches in diameter. You will

get twenty-four level scoops from a quart of ice cream using this dipper.)
• Never shovel the ice cream out of the carton. This compresses or smashes the ice cream, releasing the air beaten into it, which can ruin its smooth, creamy texture and appearance.

In a survey taken for Dreyer's/Edy's Grand Ice Cream, the Opinion Research Corporation International learned that one-quarter of the men they interviewed think a "typical" serving of ice cream should be four scoops or more. About one-half of the women surveyed believe an ice cream serving is only two scoops. The number of those people who admitted to licking the ice cream bowl when finished? Thirteen percent of the men, eight percent of the women.

HERE ARE A FEW MORE DIP TIPS FROM FORMER SODA JERK BRYCE THOMSON:

• Hold the dipper (scoop) firmly. Place the sharp cutting edge of the dipper about one-half inch into the ice cream, at the outer edge of the carton. The dipper should be perpendicular to the surface of the ice cream.
• Glide the dipper across the top of the ice cream in a circular motion—either clockwise or counterclockwise. The idea is simply to slice off a ribbon of ice cream, causing it to curl itself inside the bowl of the dipper. Never push or squeeze the ice cream into

the dipper. "Dip, don't dig," is the rule! Digging a hole or well into the center of the carton will cause the thin layer of ice cream that remains on the inside walls to turn icy and gummy.

- You should move the dipper using the muscles in your arm and back, not your wrist.
- As soon as you have a ball of ice cream, move the dipper under it, scooping or turning it upward. Then lift the scoop straight up.
- Turn the bowl of the dipper upside down so the ice cream plops nicely into your serving dish.
- For ice cream cones, hold the dipperful of ice cream upright, then turn the cone upside down. Push it gently onto the ball of ice cream. Then, turn both the dipper and the cone upright and lift off the dipper. (Scooping onto a cone this way keeps the fresh, crisp cone from breaking.)

William Clewell, owner of a soda fountain in Reading, Pennsylvania, invented the first mechanical ice cream scoop in 1876. Before that time, ice cream was served using a large spoon. Clewell's scoop, described as an "ice cream measure and mold," was made of tin and steel. It had a cone shape with a little key on top that turned the scraper or dipper. This caused the ice cream, after it was scooped, to drop easily onto a plate. Two hands were needed to operate the scoop: one to hold the handle, the other to turn the release key. Scoops using this design were popular until the end of the nineteenth century.

The shades of night were falling fast
The child had gone to sleep at last,
We knew that now no more he'd weep,
But still he murmured in his sleep:
"Oh, you ice cream!"

A pint that night alone he ate;
We feared next day he'd "pay the freight."
He woke next morn, sat up in bed,
And yelling lustily he said:
"Oh, you ice cream!"

The moral now is simply told—
Ice cream is good for young and old.
To make ice cream is quite a fuss,
But that's our business. Call on us.
"Oh, you ice cream!"

—anonymous poem on a menu at the annual dinner
   sponsored by the New England Ice Cream
   Manufacturers Association, January 19, 1916.

Many children in the 1950s dreamed of growing up to be a Good Humor Man.

Photo credit: Courtesy Good Humor–Breyers

Suggested Reading

Cobb, Vicki. *The Scoop on Ice Cream.* Little, Brown & Co. Boston: 1985.

Dickson, Paul. *The Great American Ice Cream Book.* Atheneum. New York: 1972.

Greenberg, Keith. *Ben & Jerry: Ice Cream for Everyone!* Blackbirch. 1994.

Funderburg, Ann Cooper. *Chocolate, Strawberry and Vanilla: A History of American Ice Cream.* Bowling Green State University Popular Press. Bowling Green, Ohio: 1995.

Liddell, Caroline and Weir, Robin. *Frozen Desserts.* St. Martin's Press. New York: 1995.

Mitgutsche, Ali. *From Milk to Ice Cream.* Carolrhoda. Minneapolis: 1981.

Neimark, Jill. *Ice Cream.* Hastings House. New York: 1986.

"Scoops for Schools": A Cross-Curriculum Learning Packet. Dreyer's Grand Ice Cream, Inc. Oakland, CA: 1993.

Wulffson, Don L. *The Kid Who Invented the Popsicle.* Cobblehill Books. New York: 1997.

Permissions

INDEX